Who's on First?

FINDING TRUE FULFILLMENT IN THE CRUSH OF LIFE

Everett Leadingham, Editor

Though this book is designed for group study, it is also intended for personal enjoyment and spiritual growth. A leader's guide is available from your local bookstore or your publisher.

Beacon Hill Press of Kansas City
Kansas City, Missouri

Editor: Everett Leadingham
Assistant Editor: Charlie L. Yourdon
Executive Editor: Randy Cloud
Editorial Committee: Philip Baisley, Randy Cloud, Everett Lead-
ingham, Bill Manning, Tom Mayse, Kelly Trennepohl, Charlie L.
Yourdon

Copyright 1999
by Beacon Hill Press of Kansas City

ISBN: 083-411-8114

Printed in the
United States of America

Cover design: Kevin Williamson
Cover photo: CORBIS/Annie Griffiths Belt

10   9   8   7   6   5   4   3   2   1

Contents

Preface

Through the act and process of ordination, the Church has historically set apart certain persons who have been called of God and examined by the Church. These persons are called "ordained ministers" and are responsible within the context of the Church for "Word, sacrament, and order."

That means, minimally, they are responsible for preaching, administering baptism and Communion, and seeing that the church is organized and operated in an orderly fashion so that the gospel will be spread among all people.

Does that mean that those whom the Church has ordained are responsible for everything that must happen in ministry? No. As Christians, lay (i.e., "unordained") believers are called to be those who serve others in the name of Christ as well.

In a perfect world, ordained ministers and laypersons would work tirelessly together and do absolutely everything to spread the gospel of Jesus Christ. Ours is not a perfect world, and it is *time* that makes the difference. Ordained persons are set apart to do full-time ministry. Laypersons who sincerely want to be of service find that their full-time responsibilities may not leave much, if any, time for ministry. So for laypersons, ministry becomes a matter of setting priorities.

This is not a book that will heap guilt on the reader, causing him or her to squeeze another "helping" activity into an already overcrowded calendar. Instead, we will take a serious look at the ministry already happening—but maybe not recognized as ministry—as well as those activities that may need to be reevaluated. We will look closely at a variety of topics that affect how we spend our lives in service to others—including the role and importance of laypersons in the Church, how we live our lives and spend our money, and how we find the unique gifts God gives to each of us.

This book will help us arrange our priorities to be effectively involved in the work God calls all Christians to do. It will help us faithfully answer the most important question for every believer: *Who's ~~on~~ First?*

CHAPTER 1

A Sunday Morning Meditation

by H. Ray Dunning

One of my ancestors, John Donne, became famous for saying, "No man is an island." Not as famous, but widely quoted among Wesleyan Christians, is Reuben Welch's book title *We Really Do Need Each Other.* One of my former teachers in college used to say to people who thought they could live as if they were free from responsibility to others, "Remember, the world is chiefly populated by other people." However, long before any of these folk recognized the interdependent character of human life, the Bible expressed it too.

In fact, the Bible teaches that God made us this way. If we will read carefully the creation narratives in Genesis 1—2, we will find that the Lord created humans "in his own image" (1:27). There have been all kinds of theories as to what this means, but the biblical text itself seems to emphasize the fact that part of what it means to be in God's image is to be a social being. Look particularly at verse 26, where God says, "Let us make man in our image, in our likeness." Isn't it interesting that God should refer to himself by plural pronouns? And in carrying out what He proposed to himself, He created "them"—Adam and Eve. This implies that we were created for community,

9

that we cannot be fully personal except in relation to other human beings.

That seems to be why God brought into being "a people that are his very own" (Titus 2:14). First there was Israel, and now there is the Church. God always had in view a community that would be His agents to carry out His work in the world.

I have to remind myself of this fact almost every Sunday morning. Many people don't have trouble getting out of bed in the morning, but I do. If I listened to my body, I would stay there long past the rising time to get to Sunday School and church. It would be so much easier, my bones tell me, to remain between the sheets a while longer rather than getting up and doing all the things necessary in order to go to the place where God's people gather for study and worship. I could simply slip on my bathrobe, brew myself a pot of coffee, flip on the television, and be a spectator to a service.

Think of what I would miss! It is not merely that I would be ignoring the exhortation of the writer to the Hebrews: "Let us not give up meeting together, as some are in the habit of doing, but let us encourage one another" (10:25). I would be passing up the wonderful opportunity to experience the presence of Christ with His people. Remember, He promised that "where two or three come together in my name, there am I with them" (Matthew 18:20). That isn't a promise made to encourage an otherwise discouraged small group of worshipers; it is a promise of Jesus' presence when His people congregate, whatever the size.

It certainly is not true that God cannot be with me when I am alone. I wouldn't suggest that one could not gather some blessings from listening to and/or watching a religious program while sitting in the living room or driving along in the automobile. But, as one membership ritual wisely says,

The privileges and blessings that we have in association together in the Church of Jesus Christ are very sacred and precious. There is in it such hallowed fellowship as cannot otherwise be known.

There is such helpfulness with brotherly watch care and counsel as can be found only in the Church.

There is the godly care of pastors, with the teachings of the Word; and the helpful inspiration of social worship. And there is cooperation in service, accomplishing that which cannot otherwise be done.*

I like that last sentence. No matter how alone I might like to be in my religious life, I always seem to remember the concluding words of Matthew's Gospel. He reports the resurrected Christ saying to His disciples, "Go and make disciples of all nations, baptizing them in the name of the Father and of the Son and of the Holy Spirit, and teaching them to obey everything I have commanded you" (28:19-20). Now how can I do that by myself? Why, I can hardly afford to finance a trip to the adjoining state, much less finance a preaching and teaching trip to all the nations of the world. Yet, I can pool my resources with other Christians, and we can delegate the task of organizing the program of world evangelism, recruiting people who are called to mission work, and sending them out everywhere. Together we can make a reasonable response to this Great Commission.

So I exercise my willpower, follow Paul's own program of self-discipline, and "keep under my body [or in this case, get it up], and bring it into subjection: lest . . . when I have preached to others, I myself should be a castaway" (1 Corinthians 9:27, KJV). After all, I have done the same thing all through the week in order to "give to Caesar what is Caesar's" by going to work. Why not do it in order to give "to God what is God's" (Matthew 22:21)?

I don't always think about all this when I go to church, but I should. After all, what would church be if it were not for other people—not merely people gathering together to form a congregation, but people who have given of themselves to make church as we know it possible? I should remember this gratefully, since many of those people gave of themselves sacrificially.

As I sit musing in the pew before the service begins, I think about the Sunday School session that we have just completed. What strikes me is the large number of people that contributed to that half hour or so being a meaningful time. We were handed literature that contained an organized plan of Bible study, with expositions and suggestions to help us understand the scripture for the day.

Frankly, I know a little bit about how much has gone on to prepare that little booklet. It all started with a committee of people from various Wesleyan denominations and walks of life. I have served on that group. We would come together for a week during the summer and hammer out ideas and create suggestions for a whole year's series of lessons. A few people took their summer vacation to perform this labor of love. All this was committed to the care of a small group of editors. They would identify persons throughout the world who were qualified to write lesson expositions, get them to commit to do the work, impose a deadline, and then bite their nails until the completed work was turned in on time.

This material, edited by those people in the office, was passed along to the publisher, where typesetters, press operators, bindery workers, and many other persons would combine all that work into the neat little booklet we held in our hands. That wasn't all. These people did a lot of additional work to prepare supplementary aids for our leader. When she stood before our group, she had ideally spent a lot of time meditating on the Scripture, studying the helps that had been provided, and seeking to organize the material to give us guidance in both understanding and applying the Scripture to our lives. I wonder if I have been thoughtful enough to express my thanks for her dedication and investment of time and energy for this service.

It is now time for the morning worship service to begin. I snap out of my musings as the organ peals its notes of praise, calling us to close the door to the week past and focus our minds upon the Lord. Can you imagine the racket that instrument would make if I had to provide my own music? I seriously doubt if I have the self-discipline to practice for hours and hours to learn how to coax those inspiring chords from the golden throat of the organ. Still, how they lift my spirit and direct my thoughts upward! I must remember to express my appreciation to the organist for the tremendous dedication he has demonstrated to be able to make such a marvelous contribution to the worship service.

In marches the choir. I wonder when they found time to meet for practice. I suspect every one of them could have found something else to do, but here they are, blending their voices in a call to worship. Well, most of the voices blend in—but after all, we are only admonished to "make a joyful noise unto the LORD" (Psalm 100:1, KJV), with no requirement for perfection.

When the music director asks us to take our hymnbook from the pew rack and join in worshiping in song, I am struck again by how dependent we are upon the inspired work of other people. Hymn singing has long been a part of the typical Christian worship experience, but in biblical times the music was much different. Generally what passed as music was chanting, quite often the words of a psalm. I learned from a music professor that singing in harmony did not come into existence until much later. So Paul and Silas, singing a duet in the Philippian jail, would not have been one singing the melody line and the other a different part.

Nevertheless, when I open my hymnbook to the number announced, I see poetic words with musical scales picturing four-part harmony. Somebody certainly had a gift from God to pen those uplifting words of praise and adoration. Those hymns that have endured the passing of time and still communicate to us arose, in many cases, out of the writer's own experience.

As I look at that vast collection of religious songs, many of which I have not yet learned, I realize that wise theologians, musicians, and publishers have spent many hours planning, selecting, organizing, and getting copyrights in order to bring this tool for worship into existence. I love the old, familiar hymns but wonder how much blessing I might receive by learning and singing those tunes and words with which I am not familiar. I am so filled with thanksgiving that I sing with full voice the hymn that has been announced. I wonder why that brother in front of me turned around and looked at me!

Next comes something in which I can fully participate. The ushers are passing the offering plates among the people. I watch children dropping their nickels and pennies in the plates and adults placing carefully folded checks among the green stuff. As I put my own tithe in, I have a really good feeling. As the ushers march down the aisle with the rounded-up plates, we stand and sing the Doxology. I have something to be thankful for because I realize how blessed I am to have an income so I can give an offering. Actually, since I had invested myself in the earning of my income, I was really doing more than giving money—I was giving myself. That good feeling deep in my soul—is that what it means to be blessed?

Now it is time for the sermon. The youngsters are dismissed to go to children's church. As they file out of the sanctuary, I am struck by the fact that a few dedicated folk are giving up their personal presence in part of the worship service to serve these young lives. And I think about those working in the nursery so young parents can listen to the message without interruption or distraction.

They are not only being a great blessing to the young people but also making a contribution to me. Squirming children seem to divert my mind from following the sermon now more than in the past.

Our young pastor has lots of enthusiasm, but he also brings to the pulpit "gifts and graces" that a board of seasoned ministers felt were indicators that he was called of God to preach. That's why they gave him a preacher's license. I am so thankful that he is not one of those fellows who thinks that all he has to do to preach is stand up, open his mouth, and wait for the Lord to fill it. One seminary professor of preaching I knew used to say that this would work. "God *will* fill your mouth, all right," he would say—"with hot air."

When our pastor reads the text for the morning, I can imagine that the congregation sort of leans forward with expectation. We want to know what this scripture means and how we can apply it to our lives in the week ahead. I'm happy that our pastor invested the time, energy, and financial resources to prepare for this task. I wouldn't want to submit to a surgeon's knife if he or she had simply decided to take up medicine and assumed the role without proper supervision and qualifications. Neither am I comfortable with one who would presume to preach to me the Word of God without careful preparation through study of Scripture, theology, and the spiritual disciplines. Being a good shepherd of souls requires more than being a deeply spiritual person.

That is crucial, but it is also God's call to all of us. There was a popular saying in the earlier days of the Church, "A call to preach is a call to prepare." The Protestant understanding of ministry is that the only difference between clergy and laity is a *functional* one. All who heed the call to full-time ministry should qualify themselves as best they can to adequately carry out this function.

It occurred to me as I reflected on it that I am indirectly indebted to a lot of people for my pastor's sermon. He was fortunate enough to be able to attend a Christian college and seminary. In a sense, I am reaping the benefits of those professors who have given their lives to in-depth study in order to help prepare others for the practice of ministry. Even those who were not so blessed still were required to undergo the discipline of study on their own, and that meant books had to be written as resources for this study. Thus, I am indebted to a great number of scholars who invested the effort to put their scholarship into written form from which others might learn.

Still, that was only the initial preparation. I can tell, and am grateful for the fact, that my pastor has spent a lot of time this past week getting ready for this moment. I suspect he has read extensively, meditated deeply, and prayed earnestly in order to bring the living Word of God forth from the text. That reminds me that I must be prepared to do what I can to give him the time to "bake the bread" he serves up to the congregation on Sunday. I cannot expect him to be an "errand boy" for every whim the church people have. Oh, certainly, he should find time to be a pastor to us, but not to be burdened with unnecessary tasks that the rest of us could do. That was the sentiment of the first apostles, who said, "It would not be right for us to neglect the ministry of the word of God in order to wait on tables" (Acts 6:2).

As I leave the service, I begin to realize that I have been the recipient of the efforts of an uncountable number of persons. Many people of this local congregation have contributed to the carrying out of that service in which I just participated. And what did I do? I attended, enjoyed, contributed, and, hopefully, worshiped God. Yet somehow I almost feel like the Dead Sea—everything flowing in and nothing flowing out. (I've been there and know that it is a desolate, lifeless-looking spot.)

Maybe I have some talents that I can invest in God's

kingdom in this place. I wonder what time the choir meets to practice. I think I can probably sing well enough to be part of this group. I suspect if I look hard enough, I can find a lot of things to do that would place me among that vast number of dedicated disciples that are making the work of the church possible—both here and throughout the world.

Background Scripture: Genesis 1:27; Psalm 100:1; Matthew 18:20; 22:21; 28:19-20; Acts 6:2; 1 Corinthians 9:27; Titus 2:14; Hebrews 10:25

About the Author: Dr. H. Ray Dunning is a well-known theologian, author, and retired professor of religion from Trevecca Nazarene University, Nashville.

NOTES
   *Manual 1997—2001, Church of the Nazarene (Kansas City: Nazarene Publishing House, 1997), 252.

CHAPTER 2

Most of Our Pulpits Aren't Wooden

by Joseph W. Seaborn Jr.

At first it startled me. It was not the kind of comment you'd expect from him. He's tall, has a commanding presence, leads a young adult Sunday School session, and is like other "still waters" that "run deep." In our congregation, his credibility is unchallenged. That's why I lingered with his comment long after he had left it. "What we need here"—he looked around the group and slowed his words—"is another Reformation. We need a movement of God that will bring back the priesthood of all believers and not leave the ministry to a bunch of paid people."

Brief words, but John crammed a lot into them. He mentioned the word "reformation." It's a word we use when we see that something has veered away from its original purpose and needs to be steered back on track. The good news is that a reformation of lay involvement in ministry is already occurring. In surprising numbers, laypeople are discovering that they can leave the roles of inactive observers in the church and make striking contributions to the Kingdom.

For many, the revival of lay involvement is coming too slowly. The division of God's ministers into "professional" and "lay" has been centuries in the making. Such chasm-wide divisions are not narrowed in a moment. The tragic thing is that the rift ever developed in the first place.

In the New Testament Church, there was no wide gap between clergy and laity, as we know it today. Every member of the "laity" was a member of the "clergy," and vice versa. Every person in the divine arrangement was a minister of God. Over time the biblical teaching of "Every person is a minister" got rephrased as "Every pastor is a minister, and everybody else is 'just a layperson.'" Yet, in the beginning the ministry belonged to the whole Body of Believers.

Clergy and Laity: A False Distinction

The artificial distinction between clergy as ministers and laity as not ministers traces to several sources, but we need look no farther than right under our own noses.

One reason for this unfortunate partition has to do with a radical shift in worship styles. The very way in which we do worship creates a false division of God's ministers. In New Testament times, the Church gathered around a table; today the congregation gathers before an elevated pulpit. In the Early Church, each person spoke in turn. In our time, one person usually does most of the talking. In the Early Church, the people exited the building to minister to others. In our time, the minister frequently shakes hands with people at the door and receives their congratulations on the "good sermon." When early Christians tried to do that with Paul and Apollos, Paul reacted, "What, after all, is Apollos? And what is Paul? Only servants, through whom you came to believe—as the Lord has assigned to each his task" (1 Corinthians 3:5).

A great deal of how we go about worship and church activities reinforces the ministry of one or two persons in contrast with the ministry of the whole Body. Next time you are in a worship service, notice how much time the pastor spends physically separated from the rest of the people. What signal does that send?

The false distinction between ministers is also reinforced by the modern tendency toward "terminal thinking." A sixth grader knows the need to finish a specific set of assignments outlined by the teacher in order to make it to the seventh grade. A college student who wants to pass a course must do more than rehash on the test what the professor said in the lectures, although it often is not necessary to think beyond the content of the course to pass the class. Too many people do not think beyond the 40 hours that will earn a paycheck to pay the bills and keep the kids in clothes.

In a culture so given to terminal thinking, it is hard to enter any new endeavor committed to "germinal thinking." It has been easy for many Christians to assume that once they are saved and sanctified, they have finished the task. However, the call to be Christian is a germinal, not a terminal, call. Coming to know Christ is the beginning of a lifetime of ministry. Instead of thinking of the Christian faith as something we spruce up on Sunday and neglect the rest of the week (terminal thinking), we need to rearrange our minds to see Christianity as a lifestyle with ministry written all over it (germinal thinking). We can never go AWOL (absent without leave) from the Christian faith. There is no use *going out* for Christ unless we have first *come to* Him, and there is no use *coming to* Him unless we are willing to *go out* for Him.

There is one other significant hindrance to the biblical teaching of every person in ministry—our language. When we send Christians off to college to become pastors, we say they are planning to "enter the ministry." If they are already in seminary, we say they are "preparing for the ministry." We talk about the pulpit as "the sacred desk," as if a public school teacher's desk were not also sacred. With such phrases so deeply etched in our minds, it is easy to forget that those persons who went off to train for more effective service were in the ministry long before they set foot in a theological library. As long as they remain true to Christ, even if they leave pastoral work, they will not leave the ministry. Ministry is every Christian's call. The people who deliver sermons, while responsible for a great gift within the Body of Christ, are a subset of a great crowd of other ministers who "serve this present age."

Ephesians 4 says that the role of the church is to equip God's people, all believers, for the work of the ministry. The biblical idea of "minister" is too big to squeeze into one narrow niche of service. It is a giant, sprawling concept that covers all Christians in all places at all times. Paul says it better. "It was he who gave some to be apostles, some to be prophets, some to be evangelists, and some to be pastors and teachers, to prepare God's people for works of service, so that the body of Christ may be built up" (vv. 11-12).

The Priesthood of All Believers

Peter's call in his first letter puts depth and richness into ministry. As he looked around at those who had been baptized into Christ, Peter saw his fellow Christians as "a royal priesthood" of believers (2:5). Specific pictures might have been scrolling through his mind. He was seeing a slave girl whisper the story of salvation into the ear of an arrogant princess as she combed her flowing hair and put up with her harsh commands. He was remembering that vendor on the streets of Jerusalem talking with prospective buyers about Jesus as they examined his wares. He was thinking of that former tax collector mentioning his new Master as he sat by a brimming fountain on the Appian Way.

His friends would stack up the stories. Luke would tell of an Ethiopian treasurer who learned about Jesus as he rode along in his chariot (Acts 8:26-39). Luke also remembered the jailer who led his entire family to faith in Christ (16:25-34), and Lydia, who did her witnessing on the bank of the river as she dipped her purple garments into the cleansing stream (vv. 11-15).

Nobody had to tell Lydia that she was supposed to "enter the ministry." Priscilla and Aquila, tentmakers by trade, never thought of separating their tent making from their Christian witness (Acts 18:24-26). Talking up Christ was part of their new identity. To be a Christian was to be an ambassador for Christ. They had entered the ministry at conversion and baptism. In public halls and in private luncheons, on dust-smothered roads and from hills like Calvary, Christians everywhere were telling their friends, "We have found the one Moses wrote about in the Law, and about whom the prophets also wrote—Jesus of Nazareth, the son of Joseph" (John 1:45).

Even the critics of Christianity in the first century could not miss the fact that every Christian saw himself or herself as a carrier of the message of Christ. One such critic was Celsus. At the beginning of the second century, he was sneering at the fact that "wool workers, cobblers, leather dressers, the most illiterate and vulgar of humankind, were zealous preachers of the gospel."[1] Those first Christians would never have thought of calling only a pastor if they needed prayer. They would have called the closest Christian. Their minister was the Christian nearest at hand.

We make a serious mistake if we assume that Christians who take their faith seriously should always and only go into a paid ministry. A Christian layperson is not just an amateur clergyperson. In common usage the term *lay* has come to mean "unqualified." You hear the line, "I'm just a layperson in this field." That hints of ignorance and unpreparedness. The New Testament knows nothing of it. The fact is, nobody has *your* testimony. Nobody can tell as well as you can what Jesus has done for you. You are the only expert on your personal experience with God. In our day, when testimonies are one of the primary means for communicating the gospel, the words of a layperson have taken on their true biblical value. If the opportunity crops up, you want to have your testimony right at the door of your lips.

Any difference between clergy and laity is one of *func-*

tion—nothing more. No special virtue or quantitative advantage rests in being one or the other. The priesthood of believers applies equally to both clergypersons as well as laypersons. Nowhere does the Bible teach the notion of a select set of expert Christians who have both a right and a reason to be holier than the rest. Without in any way demeaning the significant role of a pastor—and indeed we affirm the need for pastoral leadership in the Church—we must recognize that there is a genuine lay priesthood in life and in worship.

All Christians are called to be ministers. Their occupation is what they do to earn money for living, but that work has the high distinction of also serving as their calling. The simplest definition of vocation is that of serving God in whatever occupation we occupy.

In many respects, the laity are in a better position to minister to the needs of the world because they are more often in it. They are what the New Testament calls the church in *diaspora,* the church "scattered." They are dispersed and immersed more thoroughly in the work sites, schoolrooms, and sales routes. They meet more unbelievers, face more of the hard realities of the cutthroat business world, and see more inequities in hiring practices. They are on the front lines where justice is often swallowed up by greed. They are permitted to penetrate society in a way that the minister who serves in a local church cannot.

Because of how popular culture thinks about clergy and laity today, laypeople have a distinct advantage when it comes to their testimonies connecting with unbelievers around them. While it is not a biblical assumption, popular culture assumes that clergy belong to a spiritual caste that so sets them apart from "real people" that they could never understand "what we are dealing with out here in the trenches." Yet when Christians endure what their unbelieving friends face—and do so with grace and poise—their witness rings with vivid clarity.

All Christians need to experience two awakenings. They must first be converted from sin to righteousness and then to holiness in Christ. Then, they need to be awakened to return to that same world as a servant of Christ. In our day, we can become so absorbed in the church and her many valid activities that we neglect the wayward world. The truest link the church has with the world is through laypeople. Those who regularly rendezvous with the public need to be bearers of the gospel message, or else it may never reach them at all. If we relegate ministry to those whom we pay to shepherd the congregation, we will surely close off the link between the church and the world. Luther saw that happening. Only the Reformation saved the church from sheer selfishness in his day. Do we need another Reformation?

Every Christian a Priest of God

One man in the church testified, "It's time to move the laypeople from the back burner to the front burner and then turn the heat way up." People with passion for God and for their work make a difference.

There are three cardinal characteristics of those who know they are God's ministers in their vocations.

First, they treat all of life as sacred. Christians who understand their roles in the world do not talk about holding down "secular" jobs. As Christians, they are called to treat every vocation as a sacred trust from God.

Our very jobs are the creation of God. They are sacred because they are God's gift to us. Both our work and the living we earn from it are gifts from His hand. Deuteronomy 8:18 states it directly: "But remember the LORD your God, for it is he who gives you the ability to produce wealth, and so confirms his covenant, which he swore to your forefathers, as it is today."

Second, Christian ministers, no matter their vocation, make it a habit to approach God on behalf of those around them. They get involved in the ministry of intercession. Their actions point toward the Master. As someone put it, "Keep witnessing for Christ and, if necessary, use words."[2]

There is a third characteristic of persons who sense a call to minister everywhere. They have servant souls. The Latin word *ministro* means "to serve, to attend, to wait on." A minister is one who serves. The service is not more defined than that. Service that benefits others and advances the cause of righteousness is ministry; no further restrictions apply. To tie service to a particular position or function is to make it narrower than the Bible intends.

We are right to speak of "areas of ministry." Within the church, ministry happens when the custodian cuts the grass or dusts the pews. It happens when some brave heart supervises the nursery and another prints and folds the bulletins. The one who brings another to church is in the ministry, and the person who does something for someone who could never repay is as close to living the Master's model as you can get. *Every ministry matters.* The ones that don't make it to the reports are as valuable to God as the ones that boost the numbers.

I sat alongside my six-year-old daughter at an outdoor concert. An ensemble was playing big band music from another era. She leaned against me, pencil in hand, checking off each piece as they played down the program. At the end, the crowd stood on the grassy knoll and applauded long enough to call forth an encore. Jerolyn looked carefully at the closing lines of the program. She had already checked off all the titles. Where was this new song coming from? She looked up at me. "Daddy, that song's not on here. Can they do that?"

In our day with so much emphasis on a professional clergy, we can easily wonder if laypeople are supposed to do ministry. Don't we have a group that's paid to take care of it? Wouldn't we just be putting novice hands on work that experts should do?

If Paul or Lydia or Luke could hear us, they would stop us in midquestion. "Where in the world did that crazy idea come from?" they would ask. "Who came up with the notion of giving the ministry to only a handful when the whole Christian community is called?"

John, the prophetic Sunday School leader, is probably right. We need another Reformation. It will come when the official clergy are willing to move over, the laity are willing to move up, and all God's people are willing to move out.

If Christ does not return before you die, I hope that the minister who speaks at your funeral can say you were an "undershepherd of the Great Shepherd." Or, using the words of Paul, say you lived your life "making the most of every opportunity" (Ephesians 5:16). Because you belonged to the community of Adam, you went to your death as a river goes to the sea. Because you belonged to the community of Christ, you live on to serve this present age. Your candle burned out long before your influence ever will. Above all else, you were a minister of the gospel of Christ. Your pulpit was not made of wood, but the message went forth from your life and lips. And the Kingdom is greater because you lived.

Background Scripture: Deuteronomy 8:18; John 1:45; 1 Corinthians 3:5; Ephesians 4:11-12; 5:16; 1 Peter 2:5

About the Author: Dr. Joseph Seaborn is senior pastor of College Wesleyan Church in Marion, Indiana.

NOTES

1. J. Stevenson, ed., *A New Eusebius: Documents Illustrative of the History of the Church to A.D. 337* (London: S.P.C.K., 1957), 141.

2. Joseph Seaborn, *Love Set in Motion* (Indianapolis: Wesley Press, 1993), 33.

CHAPTER 3

John Wesley and the People's Ministry

by James Garlow

John Wesley regarded laity with a seriousness that many of his theological offspring have overlooked. During Wesley's half century of ministry, he trained 653 lay preachers. He also oversaw the selection and equipping of another group labeled "local preachers" in addition to a vast army of exhorters, class leaders, trustees, stewards, and "visitors of the sick."

The Evangelical Awakening in England of the 1740s would not have been so widespread had it not been for John Wesley's extensive use of laypersons. His claim to uniqueness does not lie in the fact that he utilized the laity but rather the extent to which he deployed laity and the manner in which they were used. No church among the larger denominations has given its laity more opportunity for service. Methodism would not have lived without it.[1]

What was vital to original Methodism is equally vital to all who consider themselves the sons and daughters of Wesley. Children of Methodism who choose to be faithful to their heritage will not limit ministry to clergy. Ministry is shared. It belongs to *all* God's people.

Much of the genius of Wesley's deployment of laypersons is reflected in his definition of the laity. Wesley's high view of the laity included clearly defined roles. Wesley did not permit laypersons to administer the sacraments.[2] Laypersons could, however, engage in mutual ministry. Laypersons could bear one another's burdens, care for one another, watch over one another, exhort one another, provoke one another to love and good works, and confess faults to one another.[3]

Wesley viewed laity as *called, gifted, trained,* and *sent* people. Although these four concepts were used to apply to that band of Wesley's followers known as "lay preachers," we shall use them here to apply to laypersons in general. These principles are as vital today as they were in the 1700s. The concepts are sufficiently universal to describe *all* God's people.

A Called People

Wesley expected his lay preachers to have a call. The call to which Wesley referred was not so much an initial call to salvation as it was a call to active ministry. In addition to being converted, a potential lay preacher should be able to articulate an inward call from God. As Charles Wesley's hymn said it, "To serve the present age, / My *calling* to fulfill; / O may it all my pow'rs engage / To do my Master's will!"[4]

Ministry is not optional for the one who has responded in faith. Every believer is called to active, responsible membership in the community of faith. It is inappropriate for Christian ministry to be described as "volunteer ministry." Followers of Christ are not volunteers, giving of their extra time. They are under orders, responding to a call to ministry.

A Gifted People

John Wesley regarded the lay preachers as persons who had been gifted by God. So basic was this to his understanding of lay ministry that he made it one of the criteria upon which he selected laypersons. After conversion and a call, Wesley looked for gifts.

Wesley recognized the variety of gifts with which God equips His people. Wesley taught the laity that they should not despise one another's gifts.[5] This diversity was a part of God's plan for ministering to all needs.

There are different gifts for different persons, but the purpose for the gifts remains the same—ministry. The Spirit bestows these gifts, not to form a spiritual elite but rather for servanthood. In Romans 12, Paul first listed the gifts and then moved on to the persons exercising the gifts. In 1 Corinthians 12, he reversed the process, beginning with the persons and then the gifts. "The form as well as the content of the two lists indicates the very close connection between gift and function."[6] The gifting process is not an end in itself. It is the means to an end, the end being ministry or service.

A Trained People

Wesley did not encourage laity to exercise their proper priesthood without first providing the training to make such a priesthood a possibility.[7] How was it possible for one person to have been responsible for the training of 653 lay preachers? Wesley's training was of such intensity that it pervaded one's total being. It was "integrated with daily life." One could not be a Methodist without understanding the way in which it altered one's function within society.

Wesley utilized several different methods in the training of the lay preachers. One was the annual conference. Although the conferences involved much discussion of theological issues, they also served as effective training centers for the practical concerns of lay ministry.[8] A second training tool was the rules or guidelines. Wesley had a knack for writing rules for other persons. The famous *Rules for a Helper* were drawn up at the Leeds Conference

in 1753 and included everything from punctuality to relationships with members of the opposite sex.[9] This list of
rules was only one of many that Wesley produced to assist
the laity in their personal lives and ministries.

Closely related to this method of training is the third
one—a proper combination of demonstration, delegation,
and supervision. Wesley's own ministry served as a model
for the lay preachers. Francis Asbury, a lay preacher whom
Wesley trained and sent to America, clearly stated this
principle when referring to the lay preachers he subse-
quently trained for "the New World." When many of them
wanted to settle down in the Eastern cities, he responded,
"I will show them the way," and embarked on a 2,000-mile
preaching tour through the wilderness.[10] The words "I will
show them the way" embodied one of Wesley's methods of
training. He frequently had lay preachers as traveling com-
panions, who watched and learned from him.

A fourth method of training is more difficult to label
and explain. It was simply the force of the revival itself.
"The process by which leaders were made was important.
They were not created by arbitrary authority so much as
designated by the self-expressed forces of the revival."[11]
Wesley structured the Methodist segment of the Evangelical Revival in a way that, consciously or unconsciously, allowed persons to excel in leading others.

The fifth training tool was that of the small group or
cell concept that characterized Methodism. Since the congregation and even the (Methodist) society were too large
for nurture, Wesley developed the structures that allowed
face-to-face sharing of the Christian life. Christian fellowship was an ingredient of such importance that he expected it to be enjoyed by all members.[12] Admittedly, this was
not unique to Methodism. Other religious groups used the
principle of small groups. Wesley's uniqueness is defined
in the *extent* to which he capitalized on this innovation
for purposes of pastoral oversight.[13]

Any theology that takes the ministry of the laity seriously must give adequate attention to training. Ministry is not automatic. It may not always require strict regimentation, but it does need structures for training and expression. Wesley lived out a theology of the laity by his insistence upon small-group fellowships. In them, laypersons were trained for ministry by the sheer existence of arenas in which they could begin to exercise their gifts.

The use of the gifts can be improved by fine-tuning. This fine-tuning is referred to as being *trained* for ministry. The gifts that God gives are tools for ministry. Training improves the effectiveness of these tools.

A Sent People

All believers should perceive their ministries in the light of the ministry of Christ. As Christ was sent into the world, ordained of God to fulfill a special *mission* for humankind, so also the Christian is commissioned to fulfill the mission with which he or she is entrusted.[14] This is demonstrated in the fact that Christ sent out His followers to make known His message. These evangelists whom Christ sent out to proclaim the gospel to the entire world were not ordained, yet they were still sent. Wesley viewed his lay preachers as being in the lineage of those "sent" evangelists.[15]

The Christian layperson is strategically placed in the world with an accessibility to it that is denied most clergy. It is in the arena of the world that the people of God can live out their calling. One author equated this task to an army that is equipped, disciplined, and awaits its assignment. The people of God exist to be sent on a mission.[16] In this "apostolic mission to the world,"[17] the goal is not only to bring the world into the Church but also to be the Church, the *laity,* in the world.[18]

Conclusion

The challenge to contemporary Christianity is to renew our commitment to the ministry of all Christians with
the freshness, vigor, and creativity demonstrated by John
Wesley over two centuries ago. This renewal will occur to
the extent that Wesley's vision for his lay assistants (generally known as lay preachers) becomes the conceptual
foundation for our understanding of laity in general in the
21st century.

Background Scripture: Romans 12:4-8; 1 Corinthians 12:4-31

About the Author: This chapter was adapted from "The Layperson
as Minister: A Call for a New Theology of the Laity," in *The Church*,
ed. Melvin E. Dieter and Daniel N. Berg (Anderson, Ind.: Warner
Press, 1984). Used by permission.

NOTES

1. Douglas Blatherwick, *A Layman Speaker Again* (London: Epworth Press, 1964), 19.

2. John Wesley, *Explanatory Notes upon the Old Testament* (London: Epworth Press, 1950), 1:821.

3. John Wesley, *The Works of John Wesley,* 3rd ed. (reprint, Kansas
City: Beacon Hill Press of Kansas City, 1979), 2:94; 7:278, 412; 8:224,
254, 258.

4. *Wesley Hymn Book* (London: A. Weckes and Co., 1958), 51, emphasis added.

5. Wesley, *Works,* 8:324.

6. C. K. Barrett, "The Ministry in the New Testament," in *The Doctrine of the Church,* ed. Dow Kirkpatrick (New York: Abingdon Press,
1964), 46.

7. David Lyman Taylor, "Lay Leadership in Methodist Worship"
(S.T.M. diss., Seabury-Western Theological Seminary, 1960), 20.

8. Alexander L. Boraine, "The Nature of Evangelism in the Theology and Practice of John Wesley" (Diss., Drew University, 1969), 236.

9. Garth Lean, *John Wesley, Anglican* (London: Branford Press,
1964), 59.

10. Frederick A. Norwood, "The Shaping of Methodist Ministry," *Religion in Life,* autumn 1974, 350.

11. Wellman J. Warner, *The Wesleyan Movement in the Industrial Revolution* (London: Longmans, Green, and Co., 1930), 257.

12. Robert E. Chiles, "Values of the Class Meeting for Redemptive Life Today," in *Spiritual Renewal for Methodism,* ed. Samuel Emerick (Nashville: Methodist Evangelistic Materials, 1958), 56.

13. L. Rosser, *Class Meetings* (Richmond, Va.: L. Rosser, 1855), 47.

14. Cyril Eastwood, *The Priesthood of All Believers: An Examination of the Doctrine from the Reformation to the Present Day* (London: Epworth Press, 1960), 204.

15. John Whitehead, *The Life of the Rev. John Wesley, MA* (Dublin: John Jones, 1805), 2:498-99.

16. Robert A. Raines, *Reshaping the Christian Life* (New York: Harper and Row, 1964), 52.

17. Hans-Ruedi Weber, *The Militant Ministry* (Philadelphia: Fortress Press, 1963), 33.

18. Raines, *Reshaping the Christian Life,* 34.

CHAPTER 4

Who Are You Really Working For?

by Roger L. Hahn

Stewardship is a slippery word these days. It is used with at least two different meanings, and we must listen carefully to the context to know which meaning is intended. What might be called the "narrow" meaning of stewardship has to do with giving to the church. Tithing (the giving of 10 percent of our income) is assumed to be the biblical standard of giving, but many stewardship emphases promote no more than some financial support from every person in the church. Often the hope lies with a few wealthier persons who might give much more generously than the tithe. Occasionally, a stewardship emphasis will ask for a commitment to the church of time and talent from people in addition to financial support.

A broader use of the term *stewardship* also occurs. Its basic idea is taking care of something that does not belong to the caretaker. In this usage, stewardship speaks of Christians' responsibility for the advance of the gospel and for the care of all creation. This broader use may appear to be simply an idealistic expansion of the narrow meaning of stewardship as financial support of the church. In fact, the broader use of the term is closer to the biblical perspective, expanding the important perspective of the narrower sense of the word.

Stewardship in the New Testament World

When we look to the New Testament, the vocabulary of stewardship appears in a group of Greek words related to *oikonomos* (OY-koh-noh-mohs). The words are constructed from two roots, *oikos* meaning "house" and *nemō* meaning "to manage." The word *oikonomos* is often translated as "steward," but its basic meaning is "the manager of the house." This *oikonomos* was much more than a nanny, butler, cook, and housewife rolled into one. The term "house" *(oikos)* referred to the combination of real and personal properties owned by a master. In fact, the *oikonomos* referred to in several of Jesus' parables was an estate manager. His task was to take care of the master's properties, usually in the absence of the master.

The role of the estate manager in Jesus' time is well documented from papyrus finds in ancient Egypt. This steward was responsible for the complex agricultural and marketing enterprises of estates. Management of slaves, hiring and direction of short-term workers, maintenance of the wagons and other equipment, care of the draft animals, and marketing and financial matters were all in the hands of the *oikonomos.* He carried on regular communication with the owner. However, if the owner lived in a distant large city (as was often the case in Egypt), the manager ran the business, with letters and reports flowing to and from the owner after the real decisions had already been made.

Several of Jesus' parables specifically refer to an *oikonomos,* who would have been the estate manager for a large agricultural business. The responsibility and authority of the manager is most clearly seen in the parable of the dishonest steward, found in Luke 16:1-13, an illustration about inappropriate stewardship. Matthew 24:45-51 and Luke 12:42-48 present the parable of the faithful or unfaithful manager. The parable portrays a slave serving as an *oikonomos* with responsibility for supervision and care of the owner's other slaves. The owner is apparently an absentee landlord but appears without warning to discover whether the manager has been reliable in fulfilling his duties. The parable asserts that faithfulness in one level of stewardship will lead to increased responsibility (Matthew 24:47; Luke 12:44). On the other hand, lack of faithfulness earns severe punishment (Matthew 24:51; Luke 12:46-47).

The parable of the faithful or unfaithful manager illustrates the dynamic nature of stewardship. It was never a matter of simply designating 10 percent of our income and then going our merry ways. Stewardship is a matter of constant obedience. Responsible obedience in one matter leads God to provide further opportunities for obedient stewardship. This parable demonstrates that stewardship will be an ever-growing opportunity for disciples who are obedient.

The parable of the workers in the vineyard (Matthew 20:1-16) illustrates the way in which the *oikonomos* was to work closely with the owner. After recruiting workers throughout the day to work for a fair wage, a landowner commands the manager to pay all of them the same. The protests of those who worked all day were directed, not to the manager, but to the owner. The point of the parable is the freedom of the owner to be gracious when he wanted to be gracious. The responsibility of the manager was to put into action the grace of the owner. The lesson for us should be clear. Stewardship is putting the grace of God into action in specific circumstances as He directs us.

Jesus' Expectations of Complete Obedience

Jesus' understanding of stewardship is not tied only to the passages using the Greek words related to *oikonomos*. In the parable of the faithful or unfaithful manager (Matthew 24:45-51 and Luke 12:42-48) the word *oikonomos* appears (Luke 12:42). However, the following references to the manager in Luke and all the references in Matthew use various words meaning "slave" or "servant." Thus, any of the parables built on slave or servant language are stewardship parables. This opens up the famous parable of the talents in Matthew 25:14-30 as a stewardship parable, although the word *oikonomos* does not appear in these verses.

The parable of the talents and the somewhat similar parable of the pounds (Luke 19:12-27) provide important insights into Jesus' expectations for the way His followers manage the resources God has given them. In both parables, a landowner gives his slaves money and departs on a long journey. In both, he calls for an accounting when he returns, and two slaves are commended for increasing the money the master had left with them. Both parables also conclude with judgment of a slave who hid the money he had received. The applications of these common elements are clear. God places resources in the hands of every one of His servants. He expects His followers to invest the resources He has given them to advance His kingdom.

The accounting described in both parables makes it clear that the master did not give the money to the slaves for their benefit or just to maintain their present level. The money was given so that his wealth would increase. The application of this is important. The gifts of God are not given for our personal benefit; they are given to be used in accordance with the larger plan and will of God. The commendation of the slaves who followed through on the master's intention and the harsh judgment of the one who did not should remind us of the seriousness of God's stewardship expectations. God does not take His expectations lightly. Neither will the wise Christian.

Some of the differences between the parable of the talents and the parable of the pounds are also instructive with regard to stewardship. A talent represented an extremely large sum of money, while a pound was the equivalent of just over three months' wages. In the parable of the pounds, all the slaves are given 10 pounds. In Matthew, only three servants are given money, receiving 10, 5, and 1 talent respectively. This indicates that God gives different resources to different people, but He expects all people to use the resources given them for the Kingdom. In the parable of the pounds, one slave earned 10 additional pounds from his 10-pound gift, while another slave earned only 5 additional pounds. However, both slaves are given a similar commendation. This indicates that God does not have a set expectation for the outcome of our stewardship if His resources have been used for the Kingdom.

Stewardship, Not Ownership

Given this background, it is clear that the New Testament understanding of stewardship is not only faithfulness in tithing. The majority of uses of the *oikonomos* word group in the New Testament come from Jesus and Paul. Their understanding encompassed the broad view that all of life lay under the claims of stewardship properly understood. Because God is the Master/Owner of the whole world, stewardship calls on believers to manage all the resources of nature and grace to advance the divine purpose. Even thinking of time and talents in addition to tithing is far too small a view of stewardship from a biblical perspective.

In Ephesians 1:10 and 3:9, Paul uses the word "stewardship" *(oikonomia,* from which we get the English word *economy)* with a much larger vision than many believers have ever dreamed. Translators struggle to put the apostle's theology into manageable English. "Dispensation" (KJV), "administration" (NASB), "plan" (NRSV), and "stewardship" are some of the words used. What Paul envisioned in Ephesians when he wrote of *oikonomia* was the management of all the resources of time and history. All the resources of heaven and earth are to be used by the Church to bring the preaching of the gospel to its glorious climax when Christ returns. Worrying about giving one-tenth of our income or how many hours we should spend in the church building will not even begin to accomplish Paul's grand vision. The real goal of stewardship is to use every resource available on this earth and from God to accomplish His ultimate will of proclaiming the gospel to every human being on earth.

The problem with a "tithing, time, and talents" approach is that it begins with the assumption that money, time, and abilities are things that belong to us, and we can choose to use them as we wish. Because we perceive that these resources belong to us, we must use them responsibly to accomplish the goals we believe most important. Further, because everybody has his or her own money, time, and abilities, everybody is responsible for the use of his or her own resources. Stewardship then becomes a highly private matter.

The New Testament perspective begins with the assumption that all money, time, and talents belong to God. He apportions these gifts to people in general and believers in particular as He wills (Romans 12:3; 1 Corinthians 12:4-11). Believers are then called upon to manage these resources to accomplish the goals of God's business, the salvation of the world. Since they are really God's resources, stewardship includes the management of all the resources of nature and grace. Thus, we are accountable for our use of the resources of the secular world, the gifts and graces of all believers, and the resources of nature.

This is not license for one individual believer to control the money, time, and talents of other believers for his or her own agenda (even in ministry). Rather, all believers are called to envision the way in which all the resources of nature, the world, and the Church can be used to advance the gospel. That vision obviously makes the most significant demands on the resources most directly available to believers—the time, talents, and money that we are accustomed to calling our own.

Stewardship as Trusting God

If all the resources belong to God and are to be managed for His purposes rather than our own, many modern people will ask, "Who will take care of us if we spend all our time taking care of God's goals?" Jesus answers this question in the Sermon on the Mount in Matthew 6:25-34. His instructions specifically state that His followers are not to worry about food or clothing. With the little parables about the birds of the air and the lilies of the field, Jesus makes it clear that God would take care of those who follow Him. One of the concluding commands of that passage is to "seek first his kingdom and his righteousness, and all these things will be given to you as well" (v. 33). Part of the assumption of the cultural world in which Jesus lived was that the master would take care of the servants and managers. One of the fundamental tests of faith is whether or not we trust God to provide for our needs if we launch out into the faith journey of living as managers of His resources rather than the owner of our own possessions.

Trusting God to care for us when we become managers of His resources should not be too difficult. After all, God has already been very generous to most of us. Over 90 percent of the world's resources of food, medical help, and material wealth is in the hands of less than one-third of the world's population. For those of us who live in North America or Western Europe or who are in the middle class in any culture, God has allowed 90 percent of all the resources of the world to come into our hands. The lack of food, medical resources, security, opportunities, and hope in two-thirds of the world is clear evidence that we have a lot of new work to do in the management of God's resources. Unless we are ready to declare that God loves only one-third of the world, we must accept responsibility for seeing to it that the resources He has given us are used in a way that conforms to His will for the whole world and advances the gospel throughout the world. To hoard God's resources to ourselves is the very opposite of good stewardship. It also is clearly a matter of trusting in ourselves rather than trusting in God.

Conclusion

The biblical understanding of stewardship was driven home to me a number of years ago. I had been invited to interview for a faculty position at a church college about 600 miles from our home. Neither my wife nor I had ever been in that part of the country, let alone on that campus, but the college was offering to fly only me to the interview. When this came to the attention of one of my spiritual mentors in the church, he responded quickly by offering to let me drive his new car so that both Dorothy and I could visit the campus. He also arranged housing for an overnight stop on the way. When I protested that I could not take his car, he responded, "It is not my car. It is God's car, and He wants you to take it on this trip." I could have questioned (and did) how he was so sure that God wanted me to drive his car, but the more important issue was his understanding that the car belonged to God and was at His disposal. And this didn't apply just to his car. His house, his computer, his education, and his energy all belonged to God, along with his money, time, and talents. For him, all the resources of life belonged to God and were always available for His work and will. That is biblical stewardship!

Background Scripture: Matthew 6:25-34; 20:1-16; 24:45-51; 25:14-30; Luke 12:42-48; 16:1-13; 19:12-27; Romans 12:3; 1 Corinthians 12:4-11; Ephesians 1:10; 3:9

About the Author: Dr. Roger L. Hahn is professor of New Testament at Nazarene Theological Seminary, Kansas City.

CHAPTER 5

Lifestyles of the Righteous and Faithful

by Jon Johnston

It was a day I'll never forget. Neither will George. Let me tell you why.

Ronald Reagan had served his final day in the White House and retired to his Pacific Palisades home near Pepperdine University, where I teach.

Soon after, the former president enthusiastically accepted an invitation to address our students. Extensive preparations were made—Secret Service surveillance, elaborate decorations, mammoth video screens, invitations to persons of notoriety.

The big day arrived. Firestone Field House was jammed. Electricity filled the air. Suddenly, we heard sounds of helicopters as our guest descended, accompanied by his huge entourage.

Within seconds the Gipper burst into the arena, wearing a royal blue suit and his enigmatic smile. The crowd erupted in thunderous applause. To his amusement, our student body president presented him with a new, sleek surfboard.

He spoke. His humor, wit, and challenging words mesmerized young and old. At the conclusion, a standing ovation seemed unending.

Then it happened.

Ten students were invited to ask any question they wanted. With trepidation, each stepped to the microphone. Great questions were asked—ones that focused on crucial policies and political decision making. As expected, clever, informative answers were given.

Then it was time for the question from the final student. His name was George. Without hesitation he said: "Mr. President, my question may seem a little strange, but since it's my only one, here goes: Will you have lunch with me?"

Except for some nervous laughter, the room was silent. Most of us thought, *How could this kid ask such a stupid question?* He didn't have a prayer to get near the president—much less dine with him. How embarrassing to put our guest on the spot in this way!

Mr. Reagan just graciously smiled and replied, "My friend, I'm honored by what you ask and will see what we can do." Thank goodness he knew how to brush off the kid with style! After dismissal, we all went our ways to resume busy lives.

A couple of days later, I noticed some students congregated and talking excitedly. It was easy to overhear. One described how a big, black limo, full of Secret Service agents, had pulled up to his dorm. They got out, located George's room, and escorted their guest of honor to the car. That "lamebrain" who had asked the ridiculous question was on his way for a presidential luncheon!

Who had asked the best question? Most students had to admit that the prize belonged to George. Why? In contrast with the first nine, who requested information and opinion, George risked asking for a meaningful, personal encounter. More than anything, he desired to spend some quality time—up close and personal—with his hero.

Bonding in Love

Undoubtedly we Christians are vitally interested in stories and principles of our Savior. Learning information *about* Him is rewarding, but our deepest need is to actually dine *with* the Lord. To come close to the Object of our greatest affection. To "break bread" with our Lord. He desires this too.

While on earth, He ate with people in large gatherings. His first miracle occurred at a wedding feast. He fed 5,000 and another 4,000 later—all a warm-up for another glorious banquet to which all Christians are invited. Revelation 19:9 whets our appetite with these words: "Blessed are those who are invited to the wedding supper of the Lamb!"

Probably more often than not, our Lord's dining occurred in more primitive settings, occasions when He could come close to individuals—when He could challenge their minds, probe their hearts, and study their reactions.

He ate with individuals having deep spiritual needs (for example, Zacchaeus in Luke 19). Obviously annoyed, the Pharisees repeatedly asked His disciples: "Why does your teacher eat with tax collectors and 'sinners'?" (Matthew 9:11). Because He clearly saw the redemptive potential of breaking bread together. So should we.

He also dined with believers (for example, two persons on the road to Emmaus in Luke 24). We need only recall His elaborate preparations for the Last Supper with His disciples. What incredible intimacy was felt around that table!

Indeed, dining played a big part in our Savior's ministry. Beside the seashore. On hillsides. In homes. What would we give to have shared a meal with Him? Well, we can.

Unfold the Napkin

In a real sense, being close to Jesus through prayer, Bible reading, and obedience, *is* "dining" with Him. Our spirits are fed as we reaffirm our love in these ways.

Jesus underscored this idea when, after being urged to eat, He told His disciples: "I have food to eat that you know nothing about. . . . My food . . . is to do the will of him who sent me and to finish his work" (John 4:32, 34).

Furthermore, such nourishing closeness is the essence of our Christian life. Perhaps nothing more aptly describes who we are than persons who derive their greatest fulfillment and satisfaction from being in close fellowship with our Lord. With the One who considers us to be more like "friends" than mere servants (John 15:15).

If we believe this to be true, it closely follows that our life choices will be based on a simple rule: *Everything that draws us closer to Jesus will be embraced, and all that pushes us away will be rejected.*

This will result when we allow ourselves to be drawn ever closer to Him. Our lifestyles will increasingly conform to His likeness (Romans 8:29). This will occur spontaneously, just as an egg hatches when an incubator reaches and remains at the right temperature.

Furthermore, there will be a spillover effect that has a dynamic impact on every area of our lives. We'll become much less vulnerable to the societal diseases that wreak havoc on people around us.

Let's examine three such areas.

Isolated or Interconnected?

Being close to Jesus results in our being unified—in community—with spiritual brothers and sisters. Without forcing ourselves into a single mold, we discover that we're making similar life choices. Thus, we identify together and increasingly feel interconnected.

Furthermore, we grow together in Him. God's Word employs rich imagery to underscore this point. John 15 speaks of our being "branches" drawing sustenance from the "true vine," Jesus Christ. Paul, in Ephesians, uses the body as his point of reference: "We will in all things grow up into him who is the Head, that is, Christ. From him the whole body, joined and held together by every supporting ligament, grows and builds itself up in love, as each part does its work" (4:15-16).

I have a preference for the "bridge" analogy. The Latin word for "priest" is *pontiff,* meaning "bridge builder." Since God's Word tells us we're priests, we're compelled to connect. To reach out and bear one another's burdens. To continuously affirm and encourage one another in love.

The society around us trumpets a radical individualism. Humanistic psychologists advise us to grope for self-fulfillment, self-realization, and self-esteem. Their clarion call is: "To thyself be true!" And it has been heard.

A list of "The Commandments of Me" typifies the credo of today's average North American citizen.

1. *You* shall express *your* feelings, no matter who gets hurt.
2. *You* shall grow and let nothing stand in *your* way.
3. *You* shall never let anyone tell *you* how to live, unless he or she is a self-actualized person who gives off "positive energy."
4. *You* shall not let anyone criticize *your* "trip."
5. *You* shall understand *your* basic personality make-up and then give in to it.
6. *You* shall not repress *your* anger but locate and express it as often as possible.
7. *You* shall break off all relationships when they are no longer helping *you* grow.
8. *You* shall enjoy your sexuality whenever *you* feel it, which is at all times.
9. *You* shall not steal, unless it is from a repressive person or institution.
10. *You* shall always make sure *you* have enough space, even if it means stiff-arming someone.[1]

Inherent in this viewpoint is distrust of others, and wall building is seen as necessary for survival.

What are the results of me-centeredness? These traits seem dominant:

- living for the present (feeling tomorrow may never come)
- craving for consumption (lacking inner resources)
- feeding on others' applause (performing constantly)
- charming people to manipulate them (deceiving with no guilt)
- lacking emotional depth (having repeated flare-ups)
- losing at the game of "love" (vacillating between idealization and devaluation of others)
- demanding unearned favors (insisting on unfair advantages)
- buying into fantasy (pretending and denying reality)

Excessive self-love, inevitably, leads to emptiness and loneliness, a most excruciating fact largely ignored today. Perhaps that is why depression and frustration are so rampant.

It is natural and normal to desire true, trustworthy, and caring friends. God made us that way. How can this legitimate need be best satisfied? By drawing as close as possible to Jesus and connecting with those who are doing the same. Such spiritual bonding is lasting and always trustworthy.

What is another area of our lives that receives great benefit from our remaining close to our Savior?

Monotony or Ministry?

Growing increasingly close to our Master has tremendous and far-reaching implications for our occupations and vocations. We see that our primary task is to reveal Christ, to showcase Him to a cynical but searching world. How do we reveal Him? Through what we *do* and, even more important, by who we *are.* This is true, even if we are unemployed, retired, or involved in schooling or leisure-time pursuits.

Admittedly, our secular jobs supply money and re-sources to fulfill our Christian stewardship. Wesley's adage is true: We should seek to make more, in order to save more, in order to give more. Still, a big red flag must be waved. Money must not become our primary focus. Fur-thermore, as James emphatically instructs (chapter 2), the moneyed among us must not receive favoritism or spe-cial recognition.

In addition, as laypersons, it is crucial that we see and judge our jobs from a biblical frame of reference. First, we can have a lay vocation (i.e., profession) with a "calling" just as biblically valid as a calling received by any who are ordained. I must admit, that perspective has invigorated me in my role as professor at a Christian university.

Second, even if our secular job is an occupation (in contrast to a vocation), we must still consider it a true ministry. It is just as valuable in God's sight. Put simply, in both we are put there to serve—to link people and their needs to the Source of all hope and help.

For all of us, the closer we get to Christ, the more we re-alize that ministers are who we all *are;* jobs are what we *do.* This fact is especially helpful when jobs are less than ideal. We can feel that they are nerve-racking or monotonous— "treadmills" that we must run in order to keep the "wolf of destitution" from our front doors. Or our employment can be so all-consuming in its demands of time and energy that family and church involvement are greatly impaired. It can seem nearly impossible to order our priorities.

Obviously, it can become very difficult for us to envi-sion how laboring in such jobs is consistent with being ef-fective Christians—much less ministers. Nevertheless, we must continually remind ourselves that we are, indeed, ministers and providentially positioned in jobs so that we might witness by word and example. The closer we com-mune with our Lord, the greater these facts will impact our consciousness and guide our actions. Eventually, even the worst jobs will seem much more tolerable—perhaps, even a tad challenging and exciting—because the lowly Carpenter of Galilee provides them with spiritual significance and purpose.

Greed or Generosity?

In our grabbing, grasping world, many seem driven to maximize personal advantage. That's why people pass recklessly in order to be one car closer at the next red light. Or why medical students sabotage peers' lab manuals to gain tactical advantage.

Yet, there is good news! Intimate fellowship with our Lord provides us with a sharply contrasting attitude, one that finds its greatest satisfaction in giving generously. Thoughts of self-gain are willingly subordinated, and even relinquished, to see others' needs met.

Impacted by His Spirit and impressed by His image, we begin to live out Paul's admonition in Philippians 2: "Do nothing out of selfish ambition or vain conceit, but in humility consider others better than yourselves" (v. 3). Accompanying this attitude is one that places people ahead of possessions. In short, materialism begins to loosen its deadly grip on our lives. Instead, we start cultivating a simplified lifestyle. Richard Foster nails down five of its most evident characteristics for today:

- Buying things for their usefulness rather than for their status.
- Rejecting things that are likely to produce an addiction.
- Developing a natural habit of giving things away, with no strings attached or recognition and reciprocation expected.
- Refusing to be propagandized by "custodians of modern gadgetry."
- Learning to enjoy things without owning them (for example, God's creation).[2]

Paul strongly advised the adoption of such a lifestyle in 1 Timothy 6. He begins by explaining that we can't take wealth with us: "For we brought nothing into the world, and we can take nothing out of it" (v. 7). Then in the next verse, he advises contentment (employing a Greek term that means being independent of external things). Paul concludes by warning Timothy that passion for wealth and consumer goods leads to "destruction" (v. 9), "for the love of money is a root of all kinds of evil" (v. 10).

Are possessions wrong to have? No, but it *is* wrong to allow them to rule us. To care a lot about them. To not share them. To trust them in the place of God. When any of these occur, possessions become blinders that shield us from the Son.

The pull toward materialism is strong. One might even consider it an undertow. Society makes the motivation to amass goods seem paramount to all else, a philosophy encapsulated by the bumper sticker that proclaims: "The one who dies with the most toys wins!"

The corrective does not come through bite-the-bullet determination and sheer willpower. The disease is too multifaceted and complex for that. The master deceiver, Satan himself, whose cleverness entraps and imprisons, propagates it.

Our only antidote is found, once again, in coming closer to Jesus. Falling deeper in love with Him. Submitting and committing more and more of ourselves to His will and purpose. Then greed, materialism, discontentment, and the desire to be better than others will drop off like pieces of hot lead. It's all based on the depth and intensity of our relationship with Him—because we choose to respond to His open, loving invitation to "come and dine" (John 21:12, KJV).

He Gives Us Coherence

The three challenges we have posed—developing authentic interconnectedness, seeing ourselves as true ministers, and cultivating loving generosity—may seem insurmountable. Ideal but not realistic. Noble but not really achievable.

To be honest, they *are* insurmountable and unachievable—without being close to Jesus. He is our Sustainer, the One who keeps us from lapsing into lives of futility and defeat. If we remain in close fellowship with Him "in a crooked and depraved generation," we will "shine like stars in the universe" (Philippians 2:15).

We are tempted to substitute many things for drawing near to Him. Things that fill our schedules and exhaust our energies. Church-related activities. Worthwhile duties. Strict codes of conduct. Benevolence. Not that these should be ignored. Rather than being our primary focus, they must become spontaneous results of our closeness with Him. It starts with an ever-intensifying response to His love so that His presence begins to be keenly felt in whatever we do and wherever we go. It results in our innermost beings increasingly yearning for conformity to His glorious image.

Suddenly, we realize that we have tapped into the Source, the only solution for living a truly victorious life. We notice that all facets of our earthly existence begin to align and assume right priorities. No longer do we feel victimized, fearful, disjointed, or on a slippery slope that tilts toward defeat.

One Scary Night

It seemed like a typical California evening—cool and dry. As usual, my wife, Cherry, and I retired to the bedroom, where we anticipated an uninterrupted night of sleep.

Then it happened. A long, intense rumble began that never seemed to end. Furniture and pictures fell, with glass going everywhere. Plaster and frames buckled. Utility pipes broke. Electricity went dead.

We were having a vicious, California earthquake, measured at 6.4 on the Richter scale. The community resembled a war zone. People wandered in bathrobes, door-to-door, checking out the condition of their neighbors.

As I reflect back on that fateful night, I am impressed by one fact: The most frightening occurrence was a complete, prolonged lack of power. In pitch darkness, it was impossible to avoid walking (barefoot) on the sharp, broken glass. There was no more heat. The TV, with its emergency reporting, was inaccessible to us. Blankets, candles, and a battery-powered radio had to suffice. The overpowering feeling was one of helplessness, of being disconnected.

Jesus is our power Source. To be near Him is to feel warmth and protection. His light vividly reveals truth. He generates us to obey His will. To receive these, we need only be certain to remain close to Him.

Background Scripture: Matthew 9:11; Luke 19:1-10; 24:13-35; John 4:32, 34; 15:1-15; 21:12; Romans 8:29; Ephesians 4:15-16; Philippians 2:3, 15; 1 Timothy 6:7-10; James 2:1-13; Revelation 19:9

About the Author: Dr. Jon Johnston is the professor of sociology, anthropology, and social psychology at Pepperdine University in Malibu, California. He is also president of the Association of Nazarene Sociologists of Religion (ANSR).

NOTES

1. Tim Stafford, "The Commandments of Me," *Wittenburg Door,* December 1978/January 1979, 22.

2. Richard Foster, "Simplicity," *Faith at Work,* February 1979, 8-12.

CHAPTER 6

Attitude Toward Money

by C. Neil Strait

A new convert confessed to her Bible study group, "The hardest part of my Christian walk is making the adjustments with money." Larry Burkett, in his book *Where Your Treasure Is,* agrees. He writes, "Learning to handle money and possessions is one of the most important things we can do for our spiritual growth."[1] Our attitudes toward money affect all of life—especially the spiritual aspects.

Attitude in anything is crucial. The word *attitude* means "a state of mind or feeling: disposition."[2] How we think and feel about money drives our agenda more than most realize.

We must first come to grips with our attitude toward money. Will it be a god in our lives, dictating how we live and what we do? Christians must have the attitude that money is a vital part of life, but not the most vital part.

Bob and Sue, newly married, had come from affluent homes. The first major test in their marriage was related to money. Wisely, they decided that they did not want possessions to own them and that money would not be god in their home. Mark Kelley writes that when this is settled, "We become free from the unhealthy ownership of possessions, [and] we are freed from the desire to possess."[3] When we view money as a stewardship factor with wholesome Christian boundaries, then we are free to set the agenda for money matters.

Mary is a single parent and faces the money crunch each month. She knows that unless God is in control of her finances, chaos will prevail. Mary lives by seeking first the kingdom of God. She brings His priorities to bear on her finances. David Mallonee writes, "Seeking God's will for [our] money, calls [our] motives to the highest possible level. Seeking His righteousness brings His character into [our] habits and actions."[4]

To have a proper attitude toward money not only is a good spiritual move but also brings balance and peace to every other area. For to have correct priorities is to be proactive and preventive toward the items that can wreak havoc in our lives and families—addictive issues such as gambling problems, obsession with possessions, or greed.

Tom and Alice were new converts, planning marriage. A wise pastor encouraged them to plan their finances before marriage. Months later, Tom shared with his friend at work, "The encouragement to give priority to financial planning was the wisest thing we ever did. Alice and I brought some habits into our marriage that would have destroyed us without a financial agenda to follow."

Determining the spiritual agenda for our money, while it is a good beginning, must be accompanied by some other attitudes. We must bring alongside the importance of honor and worship of God. Debbie began attending church several months before her marriage. She gave her heart to the Lord and soon led her husband-to-be to the Lord. She shared with her father that things turned around for her when she brought her life and plans under the authority of God. The awareness for Debbie began in a worship service. We honor and worship God so all life will come under His authority. Worship helps us distinguish our wants from our needs.

The shaping of attitude in the Christian's life is a daily process. As we become acquainted with the Bible, it is

clear that God has a standard and a priority for His followers. The first to be affected is our use of money. Larry Burkett writes, "Our use of money both reflects and greatly
affects the true state of our relationship with God."[5]

The Power of Money

Because of the influence and potential of money, it is a
powerful force in life. It has power to do good or evil. This
is why Jesus talked frequently about money. Gerard Reed,
in his book *The Liberating Law,* says, "Sixteen of His 38
parables dealt with [money]. . . . Clearly, it was a big issue
to Jesus. That's because it's so easy to serve money rather
than God."[6]

Money, more than any other item, will define our life
and values if permitted. It has a powerful force to invade
every decision, every value, and every dream. A young
couple shared in a Sunday School class how money had
dominated their two-year marriage. The wife, through her
tears, related how money was such a problem, a constant
temptation. Then she shared how she had attended a
money management seminar and learned the seductive
power of money. "Now," she said, "we are in control—or
God is—and we are free!"

This is why it is so important to develop a right attitude toward money. If we have not come to terms with
proper boundaries for money, it will drive our physical,
emotional, mental, and spiritual agendas.

Our values must be biblically based. The Bible shows
Christians the priorities of our Lord and the Kingdom in
which we are serving. So for Christians, it is a matter of
letting the Bible, rather than money, define our lives. A
new convert shared with his pastor that, after his conversion, most things on his "want list" had to be deleted.
They did not fit the Bible's prescription for wise spending.

Money has the power to become our god. Jesus gave us
a lesson on the power of money when He said: "No one

can serve two masters. Either he will hate the one and love the other, or he will be devoted to the one and despise the other. You cannot serve both God and Money" (Matthew 6:24). Jesus knew the potential for money to devour us, conquer our hearts, and become our god.

A young man sat across from me and related how money had been a god to his father. Money was everything. He never thought it would happen to him, but he said, "I'm here for help."

Money has the power to put us in bondage to things. It is a terrible thing to be in captivity to things. Such slavery robs us of joy and takes life's agenda out of our control. We are left, then, to the bondage of possessions. At some point we no longer own things; they own us.

Jesus gave us a word about earthly treasures: "Do not store up for yourselves treasures on earth, where moth and rust destroy, and where thieves break in and steal. But store up for yourselves treasures in heaven, where moth and rust do not destroy, and where thieves do not break in and steal. For where your treasure is, there your heart will be also" (Matthew 6:19-21).

Whatever gets our attention, our time, and our money has the potential to bind us and claim us as victim. Such is the power of money, when it is left unchecked and undisciplined.

John and Sylvia Ronsvalle state in their book, *Behind the Stained Glass Windows,* that we live in "a consumer society that measures its success not on the level of meeting basic needs, but rather by its quantity of accumulation."[7]

Money has the power to create self-sufficiency. Jesus gave us good counsel when He said, "Seek first his kingdom and his righteousness, and all these things will be given to you as well" (Matthew 6:33). Our Lord knew the potential of money to create self-sufficiency. There is no more dangerous attitude than to leave God out of the money equation. To leave Him out is to create a false self-sufficiency.

A young man shared at a men's retreat how he had thought money was all he would need. "I put all my eggs in the money basket," he described it. When a relationship that he had treasured fell apart, he realized that money was powerless to help. Money creates self-sufficiency, but it does not solve it.

Money has the power to feed addictions. All addictions, sooner or later, require money to feed them. It has power, then, to feed and to destroy. The Bible does not give us a set of values and principles just to inhibit life, as some think. In fact, all its values and laws liberate life, enrich life, and lift life to higher levels. We do not, in essence, break the Ten Commandments; they break us when we disregard them. God's laws are for our benefit, and we ignore them to our peril.

A teen shared with his counselor at youth camp, "My brother is using all his money to gamble. How can I help him?" It is a story written over and over each day.

Money has the power to make us greedy. Greed is a dangerous trait. Greed is the uncontrollable desire to have, to accumulate, and to acquire way beyond what one really needs. It is often driven by status, our desire to keep up with the Joneses. Money, if it is not tied into a spiritual agenda, will spawn greed.

Money has the power to corrupt. We cannot live in the contemporary world without seeing the corruption money creates. Behind nearly every headline of failed business ventures lurks the ugly head of corruption and the trail of money linked to it. We see it nearly every day or week. It causes persons to compromise values, to shade the truth, and to risk careers. It is open testimony of the power of money to corrupt.

Years ago, I prayed with a lady at the altar. She had returned to the church after 22 years. She told me how money had corrupted her life. She had lost her marriage, her health, her job, and had come back to "find God."

Through tears of joy, she said, "Money will corrupt you; but God can restore you before it's eternally too late."

Money has the power to do good. Before we conclude this chapter, we must address the fact that, while money has a tremendous power to corrupt, it also, if governed by right values, has power to do good.

Money is one of those sticky minefields that can create so many problems, yet open so many possibilities. How we view money—its purpose and potential—is crucial. We must establish a governing concept of stewardship at the outset. Of course, the Bible is our guide, and it is specific that God asks us to be stewards of our money. To be a steward is to remember that God is Owner. We "steward" His resources and are accountable to Him for how we handle our money. Paul's reminder is quite clear: "Now it is required that those who have been given a trust must prove faithful" (1 Corinthians 4:2). Christians must relinquish their wills to the Lord in money matters.

Stewardship is God's idea. Because it is His idea, it is backed with wisdom. God has designated stewardship, for He knows it is best—both for Him and for us—to be responsible. Reduced to its simplest terms, stewardship is an acknowledgment of responsibility. Matthew 25:14-30 is clear at this point of responsibility. God does not promiscuously delegate care of His creation. The parable of the talents teaches us that He expects competent stewardship and final accountability.

So the wise steward is one who cares for today in order that tomorrow will be safe and meaningful. When Christians have a biblical concept of stewardship, everything fits into that concept. Stewardship is a governing model. If our spending and care of money violates biblical stewardship, then our lives will reap the violation.

The Purpose of Money

Matthew 6:33 is our guide on Kingdom investment.

"Seek first his kingdom and his righteousness, and all these things will be given to you as well."

A layperson said to the church board on which he serves, "If we keep our money to ourselves, we'll suffer. God's way is to give, to invest in His kingdom." Meister Eckhart added to this thought when he wrote, "God is not found in the soul by adding anything, but by a process of subtractions."[8]

Larry Burkett reminds us, "God calls us to use whatever resources we've been given to further the agenda of His government, to spread the values of His rule."[9] When this is our first priority, our value and purpose for our money will take on a deeper meaning. Again, Burkett states, "We will seek to earn our living doing things the King wants done, and we will spend our income on things the King values."[10] The wise steward is one who handles all of life as a gift on loan from God. Such a steward is faithful to see that all gifts are used for His glory.

Gratitude is essential. The one ingredient that must accompany our attitude toward money is gratitude. Gratitude is wholesome medicine for the mind and heart. Gratitude helps us see the hand of God in our lives and in our finances. Gratitude is a deterrent to greed and a guard against an addiction to possessions.

Gratitude keeps us focused on the Giver and is a safeguard against self-centeredness. A lady who had just lost her husband shared with a Sunday School class how she had gotten through the rough days of death by remembering her husband's gratitude. He was always grateful for life, family, and church. She said she was picking up his theme, and it was serving her well.

Money is to provide for our needs. There is a right place for money in our personal lives, families, and interests. God expects a part of our spending to buy the necessities of life—food, shelter, clothing, medical care, to name a few. The caution should be that we know where to draw the line between needs and wants. Our decision, at this point, will determine balance or imbalance in our finances.

It is wisdom on the part of a steward of God to invest a part of our income and to prepare for life's events—college education, retirement, and so on. Money is the fuel that drives our values, priorities, and goals.

A young man said it well: "I'm going to do biblical planning for my money. I'm going to save, share, and spend—all within reason and none without God's approval." A financial planner cannot improve on that!

Remember the directive of our Lord: "Give, and it will be given to you. A good measure, pressed down, shaken together and running over, will be poured into your lap. For with the measure you use, it will be measured to you" (Luke 6:38).

Our purpose, as Kingdom children, is to use our money in ways that will honor the King. Our day-to-day decisions regarding money must reflect our Kingdom commitments. For Christians, money is not the issue. Love for Christ is the issue.

Background Scripture: Matthew 6:19-21, 24, 33; 25:14-30; Luke 6:38; 1 Corinthians 4:2

About the Author: Dr. C. Neil Strait is superintendent of the Michigan District of the Church of the Nazarene. He also chairs the Book Committee of Beacon Hill Press of Kansas City and the Communications Department of the General Board of the Church of the Nazarene.

NOTES

1. Larry Burkett, *Where Your Treasure Is* (Chicago: Moody Press, 1996), 7.

2. *Webster's II New Riverside University Dictionary* (New York: Houghton Mifflin Co., 1984), 136.

3. Mark Kelley, "The Stewardship of Possessions," in *A Matter of Stewardship* (Newberg, Oreg.: Barclay Press, 1984), 1.

4. David Mallonee, *Foolproof Finances* (Mansfield, Pa.: Kingdom, 1995), 45.

5. Burkett, *Where Your Treasure Is,* 7.

6. Gerard Reed, *The Liberating Law: 10 Steps to Freedom* (Kansas City: Beacon Hill Press of Kansas City, 1996), 74.

7. John and Sylvia Ronsvalle, *Behind the Stained Glass Windows* (Grand Rapids: Baker Books, 1996), 23.

8. Meister Eckhart, "Old Math," in "Reflections," *Christianity Today,* August 10, 1998, 72.

9. Burkett, *Where Your Treasure Is,* 30.

10. Ibid.

CHAPTER 7

How Much Is Enough?

by Richard Fish

How much do we have to give in order to give enough to the Lord? I have wondered about that as I encountered the following people over the years.

She invited me up to her apartment after class to look over her budget. Mrs. Smith* was an elderly widow who was taking my course on financial management. Her strict discipline had helped her live for a long time on what I considered an inadequate income. She had always believed in and practiced tithing. She not only set aside 10 percent of her social security checks but also tithed birthday gifts and extra money her son-in-law gave her so she could turn on more lights when he visited.

In another instance, students attended a very inspiring chapel service at the start of fall semester. Several felt the need of others so strongly they ended up contributing the money they needed to pay their school tuition bills.

The Andersons* were a couple who had good jobs and made considerable additional income through investments. They gave more than 10 percent with a weekly check put into the offering at church. All their property was owned jointly, and their wills left what they hoped would be large amounts to the church and missions when they died. When Mrs. Anderson, the second to die, went to be with the Lord, much of what was intended for their grandchildren and the Lord's work was lost to probate fees and estate taxes.

All of these people certainly had a spirit of giving. Did they give enough? What can we learn from their examples and searching the Scriptures?

Biblical Principles

- *Everything belongs to God.*

Jesus set the example for giving. Paul declares, "For you know the grace of our Lord Jesus Christ, that though he was rich, yet for your sakes he became poor, so that you through his poverty might become rich" (2 Corinthians 8:9). Through His becoming a human and His atoning death for us, everything we are and have belongs to Him.

As long as our lives acknowledge God's ownership, few of us will be required to actually give away everything. The rich young man in Matthew 19:16-22 did not have the proper attitude about his possessions to be a follower of Jesus.

- *Tithing*

The strongest scripture on tithing is probably Malachi 3:8-10: "'Will a man rob God? Yet you rob me. But you ask, "How do we rob you?" In tithes and offerings. You are under a curse—the whole nation of you—because you are robbing me. Bring the whole tithe into the storehouse, that there may be food in my house. Test me in this,' says the LORD Almighty, 'and see if I will not throw open the floodgates of heaven and pour out so much blessing that you will not have room enough for it.'"

Tithing in the Old Testament was part of an economic system to support the clergy and Tabernacle/Temple ministry (Numbers 18:20-21) and provide welfare for widows, orphans, and strangers (Deuteronomy 14:28-29). There is evidence that the Hebrews were required to give several tenths, not just one-tenth of their income (Leviticus 27:30-33; Deuteronomy 12:17-18). The tithe was more like a required tax than an offering. The Tabernacle/Temple was a "storehouse" of both money and food to be distributed to those in need. When people paid their whole tithe, they could expect material blessings. If they did not, they could expect bad things to happen to them because they were under a curse.

Some very helpful and some not so helpful modern practices have come from this Old Testament concept of tithing. Many sincere Christians have found the simplicity and discipline of giving at least 10 percent of their income to the Lord to be following God's command. Churches with many faithful tithers take in a lot of money for the Lord's work, as they should. However, some people seem to have a narrow view of tithing, as if they believe their economic well-being rests entirely on legalistically giving 10 percent.

Some go further, associating wrong ideas with the concept of tithing. For example, they think they are free to spend the other 90 percent however they wish. Or they think they must deprive themselves and their families of basic needs in order to meet the required tithe payment. Some tend to think that giving 10 percent and more is like an investment that will bring guaranteed economic prosperity.

When tithing is treated as a legally required tax, interesting questions arise. As a financial planner who is a Christian, I have been asked by senior citizens on low fixed incomes if they should tithe what they receive from social security. The legalistic answer is no if they faithfully tithed on their gross income in the past. They already would have paid a tithe on these amounts until the government gives back to them the total of what they paid in over the years in social security taxes.

Planned Proportionate Giving

Although the Old Testament principle of tithing has been helpful, the New Testament presents a more demanding standard of giving. The new program is summarized in 2 Corinthians 9:7: "Each man should give what he has decided in his heart to give, not reluctantly or under compulsion, for God loves a cheerful giver." The elaboration of this key provision can be found throughout 2 Corinthians 8 and 9. Writing about the Macedonian churches, Paul declares, "Out of the most severe trial, their overflowing joy and their extreme poverty welled up in rich generosity. For I testify that *they gave as much as they were able, and even beyond their ability"* (8:2-3, emphasis added). And later to the Christians at Corinth, "Last year you were the first not only to give but also to have the desire to do so. Now finish the work, so that your eager willingness to do it may be matched by your completion of it, according to your means. For if the willingness is there, *the gift is acceptable according to what one has, not according to what he does not have"* (vv. 10-12, emphasis added).

The New Testament system of giving emphasizes grace rather than law. We Christians have the responsibility to prayerfully decide how much of all God has given us we can give for others and the Lord's work. It is to be given cheerfully, without expecting personal gain. The giving should be planned, and the amount based on our resources. Paul suggested that the Corinthians should do as the Galatians: "On the first day of every week, each one of you should set aside a sum of money in keeping with his income" (1 Corinthians 16:2).

As with tithing, this system can also be abused. Some people may decide to give less—or even nothing—simply because they don't have to, even though they have much discretionary income and resources. However, proportionate giving must always be considered in the context of a committed relationship to Christ.

During the majority of our lives, most of us will be able to—and should—give more than a tithe. As the often told story goes, John Wesley gave 2 of the 30 pounds he made early in his career—almost 10 percent. However, as his income increased through the years, he continued to live on 30 pounds and gave the rest to the Lord. When his income reached 500 pounds a year, his giving amounted to 94 percent of his income!

Giving Sacrificially

Sacrificial giving does have support in Scripture. Paul commends the Macedonians for giving "even beyond their ability" (2 Corinthians 8:3). Jesus compared the widow who gave "all she had to live on" to the paltry giving of the rich people (Luke 21:1-4).

On rare occasions, sacrificial giving can fall into irresponsibility. Paul writes that the giver must first consider the needs of family and relatives. "If anyone does not provide for his relatives, and especially for his immediate family, he has denied the faith and is worse than an unbeliever" (1 Timothy 5:8).

Wrong Attitudes About Giving

• *Giving out of Fear and Guilt*

Giving reluctantly to avoid punishment and guilt is not the way to give. With Jesus as our inspiration and model, we should be able to give to the Lord's work out of a sense of joy and gratefulness.

• *Giving to Have Power over Others*

There is often a continuum between using giving to wrongfully control others on one hand and taking rightful responsibility to check that resources are used wisely and properly on the other hand. Using giving to determine what color the sanctuary is painted is not within the spirit of stewardship. The Spirit should let us know when we have crossed the line into unchristian manipulation and power politics.

- *Giving to Get Gain*

Some fund-raisers still seem to push the idea that the more we give, the more we can expect to personally prosper. There often is a financial benefit from the discipline of planned giving and the lifestyle controls of stewardship, but giving should never be intended as a method to get more back so we can live at a higher level ourselves.

- *Hypocritical Giving*

When we decide how much we can give, we should not pretend we are giving more. Ananias and Sapphira tried to appear to be giving all the proceeds of their property sale but held some back (Acts 5:1-11). This hypocrisy was so serious it resulted in their deaths.

A friend of mine remembered with great confusion and sadness a church leader reading imaginary pledge amounts from the pulpit to stimulate others to give. Another fund-raiser wrote a personal check for a large amount to be publicly announced and then retrieved it from the offering plate after the service.

Our public giving can be an inspiration to others, but it certainly should be real. In raising funds for a good cause, the good ends can never justify hypocritical means.

Wise Stewardship

As we are given more assets in our lives, more is expected of us (see the parable of stewardship, Luke 19:12-27). This greater responsibility will involve not only giving more but also learning about investments and tax codes so that we grow the Lord's resources and not waste them by paying unnecessary taxes.

- *Giving Time*

The old saying "Time is money" is often true. Donating time, though the value is not tax-deductible, is often more valuable than giving money. At our church, a group of men with varying levels of skill gave an afternoon to roofing the parsonage. I have often had the joy of donating my time as a certified financial planner to people who needed such services badly but could not pay high fees to obtain them. Part of the responsibility and joy of giving is noting how much of our time we are able to give away without hurting our families.

● *Giving Property*

Donating property that has increased in value instead of donating cash can greatly increase the amount available to give. Stocks, mutual funds, and real estate can often be donated to churches or colleges without anyone having to pay capital gains taxes, while enabling the givers to claim the fair market value as tax deductions.

● *Charitable Trusts*

Sometimes people want to give but need income from their assets in order to live. In the United States, the IRS has provided several tax-advantaged methods known as Charitable Remainder Trusts. A person donates appreciated property (usually stocks and real estate); the trust sells the property (paying no income tax) and invests the proceeds. The donor and family members may get income for life (or a fixed period less than 20 years) and a current income tax deduction for the amount that the IRS estimates will be left. The remainder will go to a designated church or other charity when the income stops. The amount of income is often higher than selling or keeping the assets because of the tax consequences. An experienced Christian attorney, with the help of a financial planner, should set up such a trust. (We can hope they will donate the time involved!)

● *Charitable Lead Trusts and Gift Annuities*

With study and good legal financial advice, there are many other ways to increase giving and still provide for retirement income and take care of family needs.

Charitable Lead Trusts pay a regular income to a charity for a number of years, and the principal later goes to the person's family. Gift annuities provide individuals or couples with lifetime income and still provide money for the Lord's work. An attorney should set up trusts, but often denominations and many Christian colleges offer gift annuities.

- *Proper Estate Planning*

Many of us have more available to give at death than we have in life, but thousands of dollars are wasted with poor estate planning. A local pastor told me about an elderly lady in his church who left over $30,000 to missions in her will. By the time her will had gone through the probate process, very little was left for her intended donation.

Living, revocable trusts can be a way of saving large probate and attorney's fees and taking advantage of the estate tax exemptions to have more available to care for our families and to give to the Lord's work.

Creative Ways to Give

Part of the fun of giving is coming up with unusual, creative ways to redirect and grow our assets for a good cause. One personal example involved trying to raise money to endow a scholarship to honor a beloved colleague who died of cancer. With the help of my brother, who is an expert on the value of historical signatures, I made the winning auction bid of $350 on a note signed by John James Audubon, the famous bird painter. We immediately offered the note for sale and received an offer of $500 within a few days. I wanted to hold out for more, but Douglas said we should take the 40 percent gain. We had fun showing the note around campus and experienced great joy contributing the $500.

In another project, I was able to raise an additional $2,800 for the same scholarship using frequent flier miles. When several individuals in the college community had flight itineraries that would be very costly, I offered to contribute my miles to get them free tickets if they agreed to contribute to the scholarship. The amounts they gave were less than they would have had to pay for the same tickets, but everyone benefited.

The Widow, Students, and Andersons Revisited

In view of our brief study of biblical principles on giving, what can we say about the three giving situations mentioned at the beginning of this chapter?

Mrs. Smith seems to be on the right track. She appears to have a thought-out plan of how much to give and where it should go. We could ask her if she is joyful in giving this way and if she has enough left to care for her basic needs. We might find out that she is miserable because she has to deprive herself to avoid "robbing God." Or we might learn that she turns off the lights on her son-in-law to show him how bad off she is because she has inadequate income. In those cases, we would point her to 2 Corinthians 8 and 9.

Some of the students who gave away their tuition may be on the right track. As with the rich young man, sometimes God asks us to give sacrificially as a confirmation that everything we have belongs to Him. Because the giving was not planned or proportional, we might ask these students to delay in order to have time to pray and review the consequences. Some of the students may be reacting emotionally to a gifted speaker, and their giving might hurt their families and the cause of the Lord's work.

The Andersons may have given joyfully, proportionately, and with a plan. The amounts may have been well over the minimum of the tithe. They failed in their stewardship, however, by not getting the education and professional help necessary for carrying out their excellent intentions. The considerable riches the Master entrusted to them were wasted in the giving means they chose to use. Perhaps some of the responsibility for these wasted resources falls on those of us who have the knowledge and fail to educate others.

Conclusion

The Early Church had a method for living in community. The wealthy Christians did not seem to find their identity in living as high as they could but rather "shared everything they had" so that "there were no needy persons among them" (Acts 4:32, 34). They treated everything as belonging to the Lord; they were merely stewards of the property. Treating everything we own as belonging to the Lord, we often need the discipline of tithing to lead us to purposefully and cheerfully give much more to others under the guidance of the Holy Spirit. We need to learn as much as we can about saving, investing, and using income and estate tax rules to be good stewards. Out of a total commitment to the Lord, we should purpose to give as much as we can, rather than how little we can to fulfill the law.

---

*All names have been changed.

Background Scripture: Leviticus 27:30-33; Numbers 18:20-21; Deuteronomy 12:17-18; 14:28-29; Malachi 3:8-10; Matthew 19:16-22; Luke 19:12-27; 21:1-4; Acts 4:32, 34; 5:1-11; 1 Corinthians 16:2; 2 Corinthians 8—9; 1 Timothy 5:8

About the Author: Richard A. Fish teaches courses in financial planning and family counseling at Eastern Nazarene College and is a certified financial planner in the Human Resources Department of the college.

CHAPTER 8

Managing Time

by Stephen Lennox

Despite all the words written on how to manage time, it really is quite simple. Time management is about determining priorities and living by them. Adopt this as the guiding principle for how we spend our time and we will gain control of time and become more productive.

Determine Priorities

Getting a grip on time does not begin with a calendar or watch. It begins by getting a grip on *calling.* We must start by determining what really matters to us as Christians, what our priorities are before God. A priority is a commitment we honor to the exclusion of other things. If winning an Olympic gold medal is my priority, I must pursue that goal in spite of pain and exhaustion. If being promoted at work is a priority, I will do my job carefully and will sacrifice what it takes to be a valued employee. If getting straight A's is a priority, I will study hard, even staying up all night when necessary.

We already have priorities. At some point, perhaps unconsciously, we decided what is important to us. We live each day by those commitments.

To learn what your priorities are, try this simple exercise: Think back over the past week, and write down how you spent your time. Use categories like "work," "sleep," "meals," "church," "devotions," "household chores," "hobbies," "watching TV," and "family." (Limit family time to when you were actually doing something together, not just when you were in the same room.)

Now add up the time you spent in each category, and subtract the time it took to do required activities (for example, eating and sleeping). The totals will give you a good idea of your priorities. Do you think your opinion is the same as God's on what is important?

We begin to manage our time when we determine that our priorities should be those God has already chosen for us. Making that decision will be much easier if we are convinced God has called us. We tend to think of ministers or missionaries being called, but God has called every Christian. Unless we understand this, we will be what Gordon MacDonald describes as "a driven person."* The driven person is gratified only by accomplishment, is concerned that others know what he or she has done, but is dissatisfied with those accomplishments. He or she sets unrealistic, unattainable goals. The driven person is more inclined to compromise in matters of integrity and often undervalues others. He or she tends to be highly competitive. The driven person often possesses a quick temper and an abnormally busy schedule. Get a driven person in a conversation, and we will likely hear only about what he or she has done.

By contrast, the called person understands the meaning and value of stewardship. He or she values people as people, not as tools to accomplish personal goals. He or she knows the importance of a vital relationship with God. His or her sense of purpose and commitment do not waver; a sense of peace and joy is abiding. The called person has determined priorities in line with God's will for his or her life.

Once we hear and answer God's call, we immediately find ourselves inundated with demands on our time.

These demands are of two types: *urgent* or *important.* The urgent requests are those "squeaky wheels" that demand attention but offer little or no satisfaction in return. The important requests are those we feel called and gifted to meet. Without a clear sense of our priorities, we will usually run with our oilcans to stop the squeak instead of doing what really matters. If we do not decide what is important to us, someone else will.

God is calling us to consciously accept as important what He calls important. As if to get us started, God has given us two commands that will determine many of our priorities: We are to love Him with all we are and have, and we are to love our neighbors as ourselves (Matthew 22:37-40). Many priorities flow directly from these two commands. Since we are to love God with all we are and have, we must spend time with Him often, we must get to know Him through His Word, and we must worship Him regularly. These ought to be among our top priorities. Since we are to love our neighbors as ourselves, we must decide first who our neighbors are. Certainly, our closest neighbors are the members of our own families. This means that meeting their needs must be important to us. Whether we work in or out of the home, caring for our families ought to be a top priority.

Since our neighbors also include our church families, some type of ministry to them should also appear high on our list of what really matters in life. What types of ministry should we be involved in? The personal answer to this question will emerge from a careful examination of several factors: What are your spiritual gifts? What is God asking you to do? What do others say you do well? What do you enjoy doing?

As Jesus taught in the parable of the Good Samaritan, our neighbors are also the persons we meet who are in need. One of our priorities should be to meet the needs of others, whether formally by volunteering in the community or informally by being available to talk to someone who is struggling.

Common sense also helps determine priorities. Research has shown that relaxation is important for mental health and exercise is essential for physical health. So we should make periodic relaxation and exercise priorities. If we don't do basic chores, our houses will fall down around us. So we must care for those things over which God has made us stewards.

Some priorities will probably change over time. While we never stop being parents, the nature of this role changes, as do the priorities associated with it. Other priorities should become lifelong commitments. The important thing in time management is determining what those priorities should be and living by them.

It is a good idea to make a list of your priorities. Write down those things you have determined, before God, should be your priorities. Put them in the order that seems best, with those flowing directly from love for God and others right at the top. Living by priorities will be easier when you can see clearly what they are.

We Must Live by Priorities

In all honesty, it is easier to talk about living by priorities than to do it. Over the past several days, I have struggled to find time to work on this chapter, even though I have made its completion a priority. The spirit is willing, but the schedule is tight. The battle to live by priorities will not be won in a day.

Before examining what it means to live by our priorities, let's take a look at two biblical examples of those who did so—Jesus and the Early Church. Because Jesus knew why He had come to this earth and was committed to carrying out that assignment, He would not be swayed by popularity or persecution. After feeding the five thousand, He left the multitude and went off by himself because He knew they intended to forcefully crown Him king (John 6:15). He knew this was not God's plan, so He turned His back on popularity and easy success. His priority was to obey the Father. When God's plan called for Him to die, "Jesus resolutely set out for Jerusalem" (Luke 9:51). Since His priority was obedience, nothing—not even the Cross —would keep Him from living by that priority.

In the early days of Christianity, the 12 apostles found themselves increasingly burdened by the responsibilities of caring for the growing Church. According to Acts 6:1-7, they solved the problem by determining their priorities— prayer and preaching the Word—and living by them. They delegated those tasks that did not immediately serve those priorities, though that decision was probably not universally'applauded. I imagine that there were persons who liked being waited on by Peter or John and who disapproved when the job was passed on to someone less famous. Because the apostles did not compromise, however, the result was revival. "So the word of God spread" (v. 7). Time management means determining our priorities and living by them, in spite of the applause or criticism of others.

Living by priorities requires us to use our time purposefully. If our relationship with God is a priority, then we must make time for prayer and Scripture reading. If our families are high priority, then we must set aside time with them. If one of our priorities is evangelism, we must make time to be with others. If one of our priorities is to teach the Bible, we must make time to study God's Word. Deciding what to do each day is determined, not by accident or by who yells loudest for our time, but by conscious decisions to live out our priorities.

This becomes easier by use of a daily calendar. Nothing fancy is required. A simple sheet of paper is sufficient, so long as it leaves room for marking the date and listing activities for the day. One advantage of keeping a datebook is being able to carry a future schedule in a pocket or purse.

Take the priorities you compiled earlier, and list what you need to do this week based on those priorities. Schedule time to fellowship with God regularly and often. Schedule time to love your neighbors—your spouse, your children, your church, and those who live nearby. Keep moving down the list, allotting time to complete your priorities, based on their importance. Do those tasks first that are most important and most difficult. Save the fun and easier things for later, as a reward for having accomplished the tough ones.

Making a checklist is helpful for several reasons. It helps begin the day, overcoming the feeling of being overwhelmed about where to start. The list is a great memory aid, reminding what needs to happen today and helping avoid those embarrassing moments when an appointment is forgotten.

I find that a list helps me concentrate on the task at hand. My mind is less likely to wander to other tasks. I can clearly see what I am supposed to be doing now. I can also see that other job is already scheduled for a later time. Writing down tasks makes it possible to check them off when I complete them; this can be a wonderful incentive. I have also found that making a list of tasks for any given day helps me to spot, even before the day begins, when I have overscheduled. This way I can make appropriate changes *before* being buried by undone tasks. One further benefit of listing my work for the day is that I can pray through my day before it starts.

I can hear someone objecting, "This sounds too rigid! Must I even schedule time to have fun?" Yes. It might sound rigid at first, but we will soon find that making a list of activities actually allows us to be more relaxed and flexible in using the time we have.

Someone else may ask, "What do I do with all the tasks I have been doing that are no longer priorities?" Living by priorities means we may have to delegate some of our work. Jesus followed this strategy when He chose 12 disciples to help Him change the world. When Moses found himself buried under the complaints of the Israelites, he recruited other leaders and multiplied himself many times (Exodus 18).

My priority in the adult Sunday School group I lead is to come prepared each week with a session that is solidly biblical and immediately useful. The other things that need to be done to make Sunday School work—like writing notes to absentees, getting the coffee ready, planning social events—can be delegated to others in the group.

"But it won't get done as well as I could do it!" Perhaps not, but ask, "Are we more concerned with the flavor of the coffee or our own egos?" What can we do better since our load has been lightened? Were our first attempts at planning social occasions all that great? How much is that new volunteer going to grow spiritually and in confidence since we gave him or her that responsibility? (Don't forget to keep in touch with the person with a delegated assignment. "How is it going?" and "Thanks again" go a long way.)

"Won't living by my priorities mean I have to refuse certain requests for my time?" That is true. "No" is one of the most difficult words for a committed, competent person to say. But we may as well learn to say it because there will *always* be more requests for our time than time to meet those requests. People love us and have wonderful plans for our lives.

Why is this two-letter word so difficult to say? When we refuse someone, it seems we are rejecting that person and his or her cause. He or she may become upset, and the relationship may suffer. Invitations to lead Sunday School, serve on the church board, and sing in the choir are very flattering. If we say no, they might not ask us to do something else.

Sometimes we say yes just because we are too lazy to

say no. It is easier to let others decide what we should do than to decide ourselves. Some of us can't say no because we actually like having busy schedules. We don't feel good about ourselves unless we feel overwhelmed with our workloads. We are more driven than called.

Setting priorities and living by them can begin to liberate us from the need to be busy. Our worth comes not from what we do, but from the fact that God has called us. Although saying no is difficult, it will become easier when we determine what our priorities are and schedule our time accordingly. When asked to do something that does not fit with our priorities, we can confidently refuse, knowing we have made the right decision. We will have more time to do what we are called to do, and the persons who *should* do the job have a better chance at being asked.

Whatever it costs to live by our priorities is worthwhile because it puts us back in control of our time. We will no longer be ruled by interruptions. One of the most obtrusive interrupters is the telephone. When we live by our priorities, we will be willing to let a call go unanswered or onto the answering machine because we are doing something more important (like having devotions or spending family time). That decision was made before the first ring.

Knowing and living by priorities helps to determine whether someone's need really is an emergency, whether the need is more important than the present activity. If not, we can explain that we are unable to help right now and set up another time. If the need is a true emergency or is more important, we can reschedule the remaining tasks and provide the needed help.

Living by priorities means we are no longer at the mercy of procrastination. Sometimes we postpone a task until it is too late to do anything about it, we complete the work but after the deadline, or we scurry about at the last minute. In any case, procrastination prevents us from doing God's work in God's way.

Often we find a task so overwhelming or complicated, it is difficult to begin. Planning ahead allows us to think through a job, break it up into its component parts, and set a time to accomplish each task. By breaking the big task into little ones, the job becomes understandable and easier to begin. Sometimes we procrastinate to avoid what is unpleasant or difficult. Setting and living by priorities means we have put these tasks at the top of our list. They can be done when minds are sharpest and energy levels highest.

Conclusion

How we set our priorities and live by them will probably be a lifelong project. Still, the heart of managing our time will always be found in this: Do we know what God has called us to do? Are we willing to make it our goal to do those things? Then begin.

Background Scripture: Exodus 18; Matthew 22:37-40; Luke 9:51; John 6:15; Acts 6:1-7

About the Author: Dr. Stephen Lennox is assistant professor of religion at Indiana Wesleyan University in Marion, Indiana.

NOTES
*Gordon MacDonald, *Ordering Your Private World* (Nashville: Thomas Nelson Press, 1985), 28.

CHAPTER 9

The Gifts of the Spirit

by Lonni Collins Pratt

Every Christmas morning in North America tens of thousands of parents stare into the face of one of the most dreaded horrors of modern society—"Some Assembly Required." The thing could be a desk, a model airplane, a dollhouse, or a bicycle. However, with the parts scattered across the floor it might be hard to say for sure what it is. Only that it might someday become the thing it is intended to be if it ever gets put together according to the instructions.

This is how spiritual gifts are. Paul wrote, "You should seek after love, and you should truly want to have the spiritual gifts" (1 Corinthians 14:1, NCV). I've noticed that a lot of people seem to be seeking after and wanting a variety of gifts. Is it possible that these gifts are already given to them, and they don't recognize the gift because it's like those Christmas morning gifts—"Some Assembly Required"?

Natural Abilities and Gifts of the Spirit

"The will of God for you is where your giftedness meets the needs of the world," said one of my college instructors. His words have stayed with me. That professor knew well that there is a distinction between natural abilities given by God and the gifts of the Spirit, which are gifts given for service to God. Gifts of the Spirit are given to the faithful, to believers.

"Now there are varieties of gifts, but the same Spirit; and there are varieties of services, but the same Lord . . . but it is the same God who activates all of them in everyone. To each is given the manifestation of the Spirit for the common good" (1 Corinthians 12:4-7, NRSV). This passage begins with an important point. Every follower of Christ is given gifts. Your gifts and my gifts aren't the same, but both of us have gifts that are given for the common good. They don't really belong to us, they belong to the Body of Christ. These gifts are given for the sake of growing the Church into the spotless Bride of Christ she is called to be. You and I don't get to stick the gift in our pocket and do with it whatever we will.

What are the gifts? Here's what Paul says in 1 Corinthians 12:8-10 (NCV):
- "the ability to speak with wisdom"
- "the ability to speak with knowledge"
- "faith"
- "gifts of healing"
- "the power to do miracles"
- "the ability to prophesy"
- "the ability to know the difference between good and evil spirits"
- language gifts

It's important to note what Paul does *not* say. Paul doesn't say the list is exhaustive. He's giving examples of the gifts that are used for the building up of the Church. Gifts that are clearly for the "common good" (v. 7).

Ephesians 4 contains a similar list: "He . . . gave some to be apostles, some to be prophets, some to be evangelists, and some to be pastors and teachers, to prepare God's people for works of service, so that the body of Christ may be built up until we all reach unity in the faith and in the knowledge of the Son of God and become mature, attaining to the whole measure of the fullness of Christ" (vv. 11-13).

The gifts of the Spirit are uniquely communal in nature. There could well be a natural ability at the core of the spiritual gift, though. For example, someone who is gifted to teach might have a natural ability for language or can see easily how one thing relates to or explains another thing. God gives the natural ability; it is certainly a gift. All human beings have abilities. The calling of these abilities to the service of the Church transforms personal gifts into the gifts of the Spirit.

The gifts of the Spirit are not always the maturation of natural gifts, though. Frequently, spiritual gifts seem to cut contrary to one's personal inclinations. God sometimes takes an extremely shy person and sets him or her in front of crowds to teach or preach. Something holy and mysterious steels shaking knees and opens trembling lips. It is the work of the Holy Spirit to empower a man or woman for Christian service.

For the Glory of God

"I appeal to you therefore, brothers and sisters, by the mercies of God, to present your bodies as a living sacrifice, holy and acceptable to God, which is your spiritual worship. . . . We have gifts that differ according to the grace given to us: prophecy, in proportion to faith; ministry, in ministering; the teacher, in teaching; the exhorter, in exhortation; the giver, in generosity; the leader, in diligence; the compassionate, in cheerfulness" (Romans 12:1, 6-8, NRSV).

In offering ourselves as living sacrifices, we give ourselves over to ministry even when something will be difficult and possibly go against our natural inclinations. The shy are called to teach, the bold are called to quiet compassion, the impatient are called to difficult circumstances, and the patient are called to bold action. It isn't always so. Sometimes the outgoing end up as pastors and evangelists, while the shy get to mow lawns and cook soup for the service of God.

Spiritual gifts are given to those who have decided to follow Jesus fully and sacrificially. In the process, our natural abilities are redeemed. God is bringing the complete person to full sanctification in the sense of fulfilling what we were intended to be. We will be wholly redeemed, including our natural abilities. God will claim some of those abilities for the Kingdom; others will not be obviously employed.

God remarkably gifts us. We are created in His image, and therefore we have magnificent natural potential. We often have more natural gifts than we can use in a lifetime. Among my siblings, for example, all seven of us have natural talents for music, language, art, and drama. We are also good with tasks that require judging of space and distance. We are all poor with projects that require an initial burst of high energy and activity; however, we have endurance and stamina. If the task means sticking in for the long haul, we're good at it.

My sister teaches the Bible to children. One of my brothers operated a coffeehouse for youth, complete with music and Bible studies. I have taught youth and adults, but the majority of what I do is with youth. I could do music, train a drama group, or put together a Christian arts festival. So could my sister or any of my siblings. That, however, is not what the Holy Spirit has gifted me to do for the Body. My natural abilities have been called to the work of training youth. Most often that takes the form of written words.

Spiritual gifts are gifts that will pull us out of ourselves and extend us to others. They most often come to us like those Christmas morning packages parents dread—in unassembled chunks. We won't always know how it's going to look or what it's going to be when it's all put together.

But we know this—no one ever wrote a symphony without learning about music. No one ever finished a hard race without training. Artists don't create masterpieces without years of discipline and work. The gifts God has given to edify the Church take shape in us as we dedicate ourselves to becoming living sacrifices.

"Whoever speaks must do so as one speaking the very words of God; whoever serves must do so with the strength that God supplies, so that God may be glorified in all things through Jesus Christ. To him belong the glory and the power forever and ever. Amen" (1 Peter 4:11, NRSV).

Ultimately, spiritual gifts point to the Giver of the gifts and not the one gifted. The writer of this passage is spontaneously moved to praise and gratitude when speaking of spiritual service.

Spiritual gifts are not about my talents or your talents. They do not center on skills we undoubtedly possess. Spiritual gifts are the work of God, and the employment of them humbles us. It makes us less aware of ourselves and more aware of the God who gives and gives and gives.

The service we give might not be the one that is in the spotlight. Paul was in the spotlight, but Barnabas encouraged him (Acts 4:36) and introduced him to the other apostles (9:27). Apollos was "a learned man, with a thorough knowledge of the Scriptures" who debated publicly, but he would not have known Christ without Priscilla and Aquila to teach him privately (18:24-28). In 6:1-7, the apostles were freed to evangelize because others were willing to do the menial task of waiting on tables. Those seven people made possible the work of the apostles—the evangelization of the world. Some are sent out. Others stay home and serve tables or count coins. Each is needed. We have diverse gifts, but we are *one* Body glorifying *one* God.

This is a remedy for the extreme individualism rampant in our culture. I can follow the path of that culture and use who I am for my own ambitions. I can build my life as a memorial to myself. Or I can follow the way of Jesus and offer myself as a living sacrifice. If I choose the first, I will still have my talents. I will have more than a few moments in the spotlight, but in the end I will have nothing that lasts or matters. I will build a memorial to myself, and in 100 years it won't mean a thing.

If I follow Jesus, I could end up in Calcutta like Mother Teresa, or I could end up polishing pews in a little church. But it won't matter to me because it isn't about me. If all of who I am is yielded to God, then He is free to employ my abilities as He chooses. God is free to use some of my talents and not others. God is free to surprise me, stretch me, or make me uncomfortable. And in the end it will matter, for it will help build His eternal kingdom.

The context for all the biblical texts about spiritual gifts is set in loving service to others. When as a teenager I began taking seriously my own call to Christian service, I often heard other people my age saying things like, "I want to be a person God can use." It sounded good, and I know their intentions were good.

However, it is not God's intention to *use* you or me. It is God's intention to *love* you and me. To serve as Jesus served, we must first love as Jesus loved. Our gifts are the tools by which we are trained *in* love, by which we are trained *to* love. It is love that will shape us, love that will hold us, and love that will send us out of ourselves into a broken world.

In a Nutshell

It's not easy to know where the gifts we are born with and the gifts of the Spirit start and end. When my college professor told us, "The will of God for you is where your giftedness meets the needs of the world," he told us something important.

The gifts of the Spirit will always turn us out of ourselves toward others. Spiritual gifts are not used for our own ambitions, but for the good of the Church. Spiritual gifts, unlike our natural abilities, might not come easy for us. We will be challenged. What's more, the gifts of the Spirit point others to God. God is glorified, not us, not our talents.

It is reasonable to expect that our God-given gifts will be used as God shapes us into spiritual gifts to the Church. People, not things or talents, are God's gift to the Church. It is the person with faith who comforts and strengthens others. A gift of faith would be meaningless without a body. It is the *person* who speaks God's Word who calls people to grow in Him. It is the presence of the *persons* that is a spiritual gift to the Church.

Rather than chasing after certain coveted spiritual abilities, we Christians are called to give ourselves away. It is in this process that we discover our giftedness and that we become the gift God gives to our brothers and sisters.

Background Scripture: Acts 4:36; 6:1-7; 9:27; 18:24-28; Romans 12:1, 6-8; 1 Corinthians 12:4-10; 14:1; Ephesians 4:11-13; 1 Peter 4:11

About the Author: Lonni Collins Pratt is an award-winning freelance author of religious books. Her latest book is a prayer journal for teens, titled *Here I Am, Lord.*

CHAPTER 10

What Is My Gift?

by Lonni Collins Pratt

For as long as David can remember, someone has been saying to him, "Have you ever thought about preaching?" Until a few years ago, this middle-aged man would look blankly in their eyes and reply, "No, as a matter of fact I've never even considered it."

He is now lay pastor for a small farming community. He preaches, visits the sick, baptizes, counsels, and performs all the duties of a pastor.

How did he know this was his gift? "I listened to the people in my life. I finally got to the point that I stopped looking around for where I fit and what I could do. I stopped all the frantic searching and listened."

Carla was a young mother when someone first commented on her compassion. "You have such a sense for how people are feeling and what they're going through. It's almost as if you can get into their skins," someone once said to her.

"I wasn't sure that was a gift at all," she laughs. "It's just something I've always had, even before I accepted Christ. Gradually, the thought kept coming back to me: *What am I supposed to do with this gift?*"

Carla became part of a team that operates a hot line for people in an emotional crisis. It is a joint effort by several churches. They receive life-and-death calls from people hurting so desperately they can't see a way out.

Jeffrey and Margaret are both retired from teaching. For most of their adult lives, they went to church and tried to live the best, godly lives they could. They describe their lives as ordinary. "But we always thought that some-day the right opportunity was going to come along. When it did, we wanted to be ready to serve," Jeffrey says. They were comfortable in a home without a mortgage and their children grown when they heard about groups of older Christians, all retired, who travel in recreational vehicles and help churches with simple construction jobs.

Margaret says that their gift is the readiness to serve. They have never liked traveling much, and neither of them knew much about construction. They were willing, though. Several months each year they now work as volunteer construction help on church projects.

What Are My Spiritual Gifts, Anyway?

Lots of Christians ask this question. There are numerous books, workbooks, tests, and programs to help us pinpoint our gifts. These resources are not a bad place to start. However, ultimately, the answer to the question isn't going to be fully discovered in the pages of a workbook.

It's an important question. "Now concerning spiritual gifts, brothers and sisters, I do not want you to be uninformed," Paul writes in the beginning of chapter 12 of the first Corinthian letter (NRSV). The members of the Corinthian church were zealous for a few of what some have called "the more flamboyant spiritual gifts."

Paul tells them that everyone is not the same. "Indeed, the body does not consist of one member but of many. If the foot would say, 'Because I am not a hand, I do not belong to the body,' that would not make it any less a part of the body" (vv. 14-15, NRSV).

Your difference does not make you any less than anyone else. But you are—have no doubt about it—different than everyone else. When we exercise our gifts, we enter into the Body of Christ in a harmonious way. Without your contribution, something is going to be missing.

Take, for instance, music written in four-part harmony but performed in three-part harmony. The song goes on, but there is an empty spot. Each of us is given notes to sing that no one else has been created to sing.

The Bible clearly proclaims the profound worth of human beings. We are not accidental, and our lives are not a lost speck of dust whirling into some unknown destiny. We were planned. We are known. We are loved. We matter.

Each of us brings all his or her experience, genetic makeup, education—the whole self—to the work of God. We are each unique; never before and never again will we be exactly duplicated. So while you and I may both have the gift of generosity, it will be expressed in each of us in different ways. You might open your home to troubled young adults, while I might financially support a ministry, a family, or a church.

Spiritual gifts are recognized in many ways. It is too mysterious a process to be able to set it up in a chart. However, there are some ways of discovering gifts that have worked for others.

 • *Listen to what people say.*

Others often see something in us that we don't recognize in ourselves. Acts 11:25 is a little phrase that says a lot: "Then Barnabas went to Tarsus to look for Saul." We don't know what Saul was doing, but he had clearly gone home after an early disappointment in Jerusalem. It was Barnabas who went after him, shook the dust off him, and pointed him in the right direction. God used Barnabas to empower Saul, who became the great apostle Paul. God will use people in our lives too.

It might be helpful to talk to someone about your gifts. Ask someone who knows you well, someone you trust.

(Don't pick a negative person; some people are not good at this sort of thing.) Ask him or her to tell you what he or she perceives to be your strengths and gifts. Ask more than one person. Mature Christians won't be surprised by your questions.

Often, though, the most important information about your gifts will be provided in the casual comments that people who know you toss around. Pay very close attention to what others are saying about you.

- *Consider natural talents as clues that might reveal spiritual gifts.*

Joanne teaches fifth grade in a public school. She also teaches a junior high Sunday School class. She knows a lot of teachers who don't want anything to do with teaching in a church setting. "But this isn't just what I *do,* it's who I *am.* This is my gift."

Natural abilities are not the same thing as gifts of the Spirit, but there could well be a natural ability at the core of a spiritual gift. Talents are God-given and provide a good place to begin the journey of discovering your giftedness. Your preferences tell you something about yourself. These sacred desires have everything to do with your uniqueness. Your natural abilities and your life experiences have shaped you into the person who is called—today—to the service of the Church.

Often, as Christians, we think that acknowledging some talent or gift is less than humble. Such an idea is misguided and just plain wrong. Humility is not intelligent men or women ignoring or denying their intelligence, it is not the physically attractive pretending they're plain, or the articulate acting as if they are unable to express themselves. Humility recognizes the distinctive gifts we are given without taking any credit for them and without being impressed with ourselves. We can no more take credit for intelligence or artistic or musical ability than we can take credit for having brown eyes or freckles.

- *Pay attention to the thing that won't go away.*

Remember Carla? The question of what to do with her gift of compassion kept coming back at her. It nagged at her mind and heart. It echoed in gospel messages, music, and prayer. She felt pursued by the question.

When this happens, it is a good idea to sit still and listen. The voice of God hardly ever rumbles and roars. God's voice is heard more often in the whisper than the thunder.

- *Prepare to serve.*

Even if the thing that captivates our souls and makes us feel as if we have found life's purpose has eluded us, we can continue to prepare, continue to remain open. We do this in prayer, in spending time with Scripture, in focusing on growing in God rather than feeling restless to be "doing something."

Recognizing our spiritual gifts means we must be able to hear God, but it's precisely at this point that we often struggle. Our hearts are sometimes hard, crusty things. Prayer will break up the shell, it will soften our edges, and we will gradually come to know the voice of God. It doesn't happen quickly. We have to learn to practice the presence of God.

That's not an easy thing to do because it means going against the grain. Our culture provides us with more information than we can possibly use in a lifetime, but information isn't necessarily truth. Information per se will not grow us up spiritually.

The shallowness of our culture infects us if we don't resist it. Preparing ourselves to serve means praying more, practicing the spiritual disciplines, seeking God daily and relentlessly.

- *Offer to do what needs doing rather than waiting for something that feels right.*

This doesn't mean rush in and try to do *every*thing. It means that if you are wondering about your gifts, go to work at *some*thing. Many people have discovered their gifts this way. The work itself may reveal something that can't be realized by contemplating on the sidelines.

That's what Jeffrey and Margaret did when they heard of a ministry and decided to give it a try. They could have kept waiting for the right opportunity to come along. Instead, they walked into the opportunity that existed, and they have discovered their spiritual gifts.

Don't worry about making a mistake or about doing what you don't feel called to do. Nothing bad will happen if you spend time teaching junior high boys, and it turns out that your gift is administration. You will have more experience to bring to whatever you eventually learn is right for you. Whatever gifts, graces, and callings exist, you will not discover them by passivity. Instead, the gifts will be revealed and refined as you work and serve. Find something to do, and then do it with all your heart.

According to what needs doing, your gifts may change as you grow spiritually. Being gifted today for one role doesn't eliminate the possibility of being gifted differently for another role in the future. Nevertheless, you won't discover how your gifts are developing unless you employ them.

Developing the Gift Within

Let's talk about two difficult situations, situations in which gifts are not used or developed fully.

First, there is Jerry. His gifts involve music. There is no doubt about that. Jerry has not received any training, though. He hasn't been to college, he hasn't taken vocal or piano lessons, and he doesn't keep up-to-date with new trends, technologies, and methods.

Despite his failure to develop his gift, Jerry remains talented. Yet, when you hear Jerry sing or lead a choir, you have a sense of raw, powerful skill that has yet to mature.

Then there's Natalie. Her gifts are teaching and preaching. However, she is in a Christian tradition that places severe restrictions on what women are allowed to do in ministry. Natalie remains within this tradition, and she serves as best she can by helping out in the kitchen and by organizing children's church. Natalie isn't unhappy, but she is unfulfilled. "I go home empty after the church gathers. I feel as if I'll explode sometimes because I can't do the thing that I'm created to do. It's very frustrating."

For complicated, difficult reasons, Natalie is not developing her gifts any more than Jerry.

Do we have a responsibility to develop our spiritual gifts—not only Jerry and Natalie, but also you and I?

"Do not neglect the [spiritual, NASB] gift that is in you, which was given to you. . . . Put these things into practice, devote yourself to them, so that all may see your progress" (1 Timothy 4:14-15, NRSV).

"From everyone who has been given much, much will be demanded; and from the one who has been entrusted with much, much more will be asked" (Luke 12:48).

If spiritual gifts were of our own making, maybe God wouldn't speak so seriously about the responsibility we have to develop them. However, spiritual gifts are a sacred trust and not to be taken lightly. Both of the above scripture passages speak of the dedication we are to give to the development of our gifts, our ministries, and our priesthood as believers.

In Luke 19:12-27, Jesus told a parable about 10 servants who were each trusted with the money of a powerful man. They were empowered to "put this money to work . . . until I come back" (v. 13). We're told there were 10 such servants, but Jesus told us the fate of only 3 of them, leaving you and me to step into the shoes of the others. The first 2 went out and invested the money. They did as they were told. They caused it to grow; they did something useful with it.

The other servant simply returned the gift, undeveloped and unproductive, into the hands of the nobleman.

He didn't do anything bad. He didn't deny it, waste it, or throw it away. The point is that he didn't do *anything*. He allowed the thing that was entrusted to him to stagnate.

Jesus ended the parable by making it clear that allowing our gifts to collect dust is not acceptable to God. The gift isn't ours. We didn't conceive of it, we didn't make it happen, but we are responsible to do something with it. We must develop it. We must train ourselves to employ our spiritual gifts with reverence and responsibility.

Background Scripture: Luke 12:48; 19:12-27; Acts 11:25; 1 Corinthians 12:1, 14-15; 1 Timothy 4:14-15

About the Author: Lonni Collins Pratt is an award-winning freelance author of religious books. She and her husband (who is a pastor) have five adult children and one granddaughter.

CHAPTER 11

Building Bridges of Love

by Mark R. Littleton

Francis Bacon said, "A man must make his opportunity, as oft as find it."[1] Abraham Lincoln expanded the idea with these words: "I think the necessity of being *ready* increases.—Look to it."[2]

The apostle Paul gave us the original principle in 2 Timothy 4:2: "Preach the Word; be prepared in season and out of season." "Be prepared"—that's readiness. "In season"—that's *taking* the opportunity when it's convenient. "Out of season"—that's *making* the opportunity, even though it's not convenient.

Taking and making opportunities are the best ways that I know to make lifestyle evangelism a reality in the lives of average Christians. Although Paul was writing to Timothy, a pastor, he certainly included all Christians in the principle. We are to be intentional—always thinking about ways to make it happen—in our evangelistic efforts.

It all comes down to a wise and effective way of doing evangelism. In our day, many different styles of evangelism have come, stayed, and gone. "Friendship evangelism" has been extremely popular. So has "stadium evangelism," "church service evangelism," "door-to-door evangelism," "standing on the corner and giving out tracts evangelism," "just walk up to them and let 'er rip evangelism," and a multitude of other styles.

Interestingly enough, the Bible does not promote one

methodology over another. Just look at this variety we see in Jesus, Paul, Peter, and others:

- Befriending people and working to lead them to the Kingdom (Zacchaeus in Luke 19, sinners and tax collectors at Matthew's house in Matthew 9)
- Approaching others cold turkey (Philip with the Ethiopian eunuch in Acts 8)
- Talking to people off-the-cuff in the marketplace (Paul in Athens in Acts 17:17)
- Standing up when a crowd gathered for some reason (Peter's explanation of the first disciples speaking in other tongues on the Day of Pentecost in Acts 2)
- Searching people out in unusual spots (Paul finding Lydia in Acts 16)
- Responding to a person's need on the spot (the Philippian jailer in Acts 16)
- Going to places where a crowd would be (Paul reasoning in the synagogue at Thessalonica in Acts 17)

The linking principle for all of this relates to Paul's words in 2 Timothy 4:2. The idea seems to be, *"Take* the opportunity whenever and wherever it occurs. If no opportunity arises, *make* the opportunity happen!" Of course, this requires that we be sensitive to the Spirit's leading, for it is He who leads us (Romans 8:14) and draws persons to Christ (John 6:44).

When we become sensitive to "opportunity" awareness, it's amazing how many different chances arise to share the gospel, in whole or in part. It doesn't have to be a specific verse or a full-blown explanation. We might simply "plant a seed" that will later result in questions, conversations, and discussions that lead to a complete sharing of the gospel.

Part of a Lifestyle

The important thing is that we implant this awareness into our lifestyles. We "intentionally" go to work, the store, a restaurant, the mall, wherever. This means we go with the intention of being alert to people who will be open to hearing the Good News. We make it our aim and desire to share bits and pieces of the truth wherever we are, whenever we can.

It's a powerful idea. Imagine if we Christians decided to look for opportunities in our communities everywhere we go—whether church or neighborhood. How would that change our speech, our thoughts, and our deeds? It would change them radically. Each of us would take on a whole new mind-set. We'd be alert in every situation for opportunities the Spirit provides in which to share.

That's ultimately what being "a contagious Christian" is all about—going into "the highways and byways" with the purpose to invite others into the kingdom of God. It calls for a radical change in the average Christian's mind to be always open, always seeking to spread the news of God's kingdom. It becomes the priority and focus of our lives. Instead of doing evangelism only on visitation night, or only at church, or only when the survey team goes door-to-door, we would look for opportunities everywhere we go.

How to Take the Opportunity

How, then, do we learn to take the opportunity and make evangelism happen in the daily give-and-take of life? Here are a number of practical ways to "take" and "make" opportunities to share the message of Jesus Christ.

Plant a seed; let it grow. A "seed" is a simple thought, a short statement, or a dropped hint. It might be a statement that can lead to more discussion.

I sat in the office of a coworker talking about a problem we had with an employee. I asked her how to handle a confrontation. She explained it to me, and I suddenly saw a parallel to the process of church discipline in Matthew 18:15-17, I told her. She was appreciative, but I added, "You'd be amazed how much light the Bible sheds on business practices."

I let that one ride, but later she began asking me questions. Over the years, we had many conversations about the Bible. Though she has not yet converted to faith in Christ, she now knows what the Bible says about many issues she's had to face in life.

When we plant a seed, we're not concerned to manipulate the situation into sharing a complete outline of the gospel. Instead, we're just dropping a hint. We're simply opening a space that can lead to further conversations. All we want to do is get them thinking. Few people are led to the Lord in a onetime encounter anyway. It's a process of many seeds being planted, nurtured by the Holy Spirit. As He leads us in planting those seeds, eventually someone can share the whole gospel with that person.

Obviously, this works best with people we know and talk to regularly—coworkers, neighbors, relatives, and friends. Don't ever think that anyone, even those most vocal against Christianity, are out of God's reach. Plant those seeds, and expect God to speak to their hearts, just as He spoke to the eunuch in Acts 8 and Lydia in Acts 16.

Be alert in conversations or situations. Sometimes people open a door in their lives that a semitrailer could barrel through, but we Christians pass right over it. We need to learn to spot those openings when friends or coworkers are making themselves vulnerable. It may be an opportunity provided by the Holy Spirit for us to plant a seed or share a truth.

My former boss, who tended to be rather irreligious, waxed profanely about an issue in a meeting with another coworker and me. He was halfway through a cursing jag when suddenly he stopped, fixed his eyes on me sternly, and said, "You know, Littleton, you really cramp my style." I laughed and took the chance to tell a funny story about someone else who once said that, with the conclusion that I'd be praying for him. He didn't quite know how to take it. However, later he not only toned down in my presence but also began asking me questions about my beliefs.

Be sensitive to what people say. A death in the family can be a time when people are willing to talk. Crises, problems, difficult situations are all times to listen to what people are really saying.

Keep a tract handy. A preacher once told me, "If you don't have a tract with you, you're not dressed right." While I haven't always been "dressed right" since then, I find that tracts are very handy. There are multitudes of ways to give them to people, but often the direct way is best. "Would you be willing to take a look at a little pamphlet about something that changed my life?" Or, "Here's something that has really helped me. Would you take one?"

Of course, with persons we see frequently, we can give it to them with a follow-up: "If you ever want to discuss it, I'd be very willing." Or, "Let me know what you think of it."

Often a tract will present the whole gospel in a way that we can't in a conversation. I have given tracts out in malls during my walk at lunchtime and then on my return lap found the person I gave the tract to reading it. If you give tracts to people in malls, it is a good idea to try to give them to people who are seated and look as if they have nothing to do. Often, they'll be glad to take something to read.

Tracts are an old and tested way of sharing the faith. Yet, many Christians spurn them. Why? Because it's embarrassing? Because it labels us as "fanatic"? Because someone might be offended? Perhaps, but remember what Paul said: "God chose the foolish things of the world to shame the wise" (1 Corinthians 1:27). If the Spirit leads us to do this sincerely and humbly, most people will accept it that way.

Of course, remember to select tracts carefully. Don't pick offensive ones. Or don't use ones that fail to get the whole message across. There is a multitude of tools available. Find ones that fit your faith and personality, and keep them available to give to a seeker at a moment's notice.

Find out people's interests. People like to talk about

what's meaningful and interesting to them. So the easiest way to create opportunities to chat is to find out what they like. Try to learn something about their favorite subjects, and be ready to talk meaningfully with them on later occasions. This is one way to show our interest in them as persons.

My brother mentioned to me that he likes to read books by John Irving. While reading a Christian magazine, I found a review of Irving's latest book, *A Prayer for Owen Meany.* I decided to read it because I thought my brother might also read it.

Sure enough, six months later on a vacation I mentioned reading it, and we got into a discussion about Irving's books. It was a good conversation, one of those building blocks that I hope will one day bring my brother to Christ.

Books are not the only way. We can also listen to music, watch television or a video, or read a magazine—all to gain an opportunity to share the gospel. A good one recently for my wife and me has been *Titanic.* Neither of us has seen the movie, but we've read enough about it to know that it's basically the story of an illicit relationship. This has led to several conversations about what constitutes morality and right values with people who thought *Titanic* was wonderful. They didn't understand our position until we talked at length about it. Then they were saying, "I never thought of it that way."

One more seed planted. If we care about a person, we'll care enough to find out what they like and show them we're interested in it too.

Don't be afraid to join other groups. Many people get involved in garden clubs, local artists' groups, or book discussions at the library, based on personal interests. If you have such an interest, join a group. Meet the people in it. Make some friends. Be open to share the gospel.

I have recently joined two writers' groups where I meet

people who are not Christians. We discuss our latest writing projects, and I try to present things for discussion that might open a door. In one group, not only have I had opportunities to show my writing, but also members frequently make comments that relate to their knowledge of me as a Christian.

Going to community gatherings also helps. If your community has an association of some sort, join it and get involved. Some time ago, I decided to edit and write our association's newsletter. It's been a way to meet people, show that I'm concerned about our community, and do something interesting and helpful. It's also a way to build friendships and acquaintances that might become bridges to the gospel.

Give gifts that edify. It doesn't cost much to give someone a nice memento or a book. If you're aware that a fellow worker, friend in the neighborhood, or other acquaintance has gone through some trouble, why not buy them a book or something else that will let them know you care? Even if they don't read it right away, it may open up opportunities later.

As an author, I keep copies of some of my books at work. Frequently, I give copies away to people I meet, after signing them and adding a scripture or personal comment. I have also given copies away to neighbors and other people I meet. On several occasions, that has provoked comments that led to opportunities to give my testimony.

As a member of a Christian business group, I have invited a number of friends to luncheons where men come and share their Christian testimonies. Two of the men I have taken have made professions of faith because of the meetings. Others have been open to more discussion. It's a way of sharing the gift of food and friendship in an edifying atmosphere.

Use special occasions. When someone retires, gets a promotion, has a baby, suffers a loss, or has another critical life experience, it's a good time to give them a special word or a gift.

Recently, I took a leave of absence from my company so that I could write full-time. I wasn't sure how to use it as a word of testimony at first, then an idea hit me. I took my last day at work to write an individual letter to each member of our staff. In it, I put a number of personal words of appreciation for things that they'd done for me over the years. In conclusion, I gave a word of testimony and enclosed a tract.

After I left, I received more comments, more thanks, more words of interest and gratitude for those letters than anything I'd ever done. Hopefully, they will also yield spiritual fruit, but that is in God's hands.

Ultimately, reaping souls for the kingdom of God is God's work. I tend to think that the evangelism process involves a whole string of good words, gifts, kindness, and gentle deeds from Spirit-led Christians that finally lead persons to commitment to Christ. As Paul pointed out so long ago, "I planted the seed, Apollos watered it, but *God made it grow*" (1 Corinthians 3:6, emphasis added). We can't all be the final link that actually brings a person to the point of faith, but we can be part of the process.

Background Scripture: Matthew 9; 18:15-17; Luke 19; Acts 2; 8; 16; 17; 1 Corinthians 1:27; 3:6; 2 Timothy 4:2

About the Author: Mark Littleton is a former pastor, now a freelance writer who has written over 56 books. He lives with his wife, Jeanette, and three children in Des Moines, Iowa.

NOTES

1. *The Oxford Dictionary of Quotations* (New York: Oxford University Press, 1979), 25.

2. Ibid., 314.

CHAPTER 12

An Expanding Vision

by Stan Ingersol

The Holiness denomination in which I was raised was probably not much different from your own. It had a fairly clear-cut identity in the 1940s and '50s. Revivals and missions were its trademarks. A strict moral code separated "us" from "the world." We were not like the big mainline denominations that we deemed guilty of theological compromise and a perverted social gospel. Happily we left their fate to God, confident in our own destination. We were heaven-bound.

Then a funny thing happened on our way to the New Jerusalem. Somewhere along the road the Holy Spirit convicted *us* of *our* racism. Our lily-white districts and white flight to the suburbs suddenly made us look like "less than conquerors." The Holy Spirit convicted us further of neglecting the cry of the needy at our doorstep and around the world.

And in time we took heed and began responding. We rediscovered the city as a place of physical and spiritual need and began redirecting some of our resources there. We planted inner-city churches that combined evangelism and social compassion. We began taking world hunger seriously, set up child sponsorship programs, and gave money for disaster relief.

The rebirth of social responsibility among Wesleyan-Holiness churches was part of a much broader Evangelical renaissance. And for once we were not the tailgaters at this party. Thinkers with deep roots in the Wesleyan-Holiness tradition were among those who helped to renew the Evangelical conscience, including Timothy Smith (Nazarene), Donald Dayton (Wesleyan), Howard Snyder (Free Methodist), and Ron Sider (Brethren in Christ).

Two strategies were employed as Wesleyan-Holiness churches began rethinking their mission in the contemporary world. One was to approach the Bible with new ears and to listen more carefully to the thread of social compassion in God's name that runs from the Pentateuch through the Prophets and into the Gospels, Acts, and the Epistles.

The other strategy was to examine how Christians of other days and places have been influenced by this scriptural theme of social compassion. Does our Wesleyan-Holiness history offer concrete examples of faithful response that can serve as models or inspiration for our own faith walk? A renewed interest in John Wesley and the Wesleyan theological tradition was linked directly with the more immediate and vital question: how should we act today? Does our history as Wesleyan-Holiness people hinder or enable a faithful response to the needy?

John Wesley and Early Methodism

The first Methodist society was composed of Oxford University students who gathered in the 1720s under the leadership of John and Charles Wesley. Their original purpose was to support one another by meeting regularly for mutual prayer, Bible study, and moral discipline, and to hold one another accountable for their academic studies.

Soon, however, these earnest young students began reaching beyond their own world of privilege and linked their pursuit of Christian holiness with ministry to the poor. They began visiting those in the debtors' prisons. In time they also met with condemned prisoners on death row, prayed with them, and—when asked—accompanied the condemned to the gallows. Soon they were providing for other needs of the poor—food, clothing, or whatever other needs they could supply.

Methodism's subsequent development into a popular and worldwide religious movement emerged as a direct consequence of John Wesley's determination in the late 1730s to take the gospel to the poor. Several months after his famous heartwarming experience at Aldersgate, Wesley followed the lead of an associate, George Whitefield, and began preaching to those who labored under harsh conditions in the coal mines near England's western seaport of Bristol.

Wesley took a series of unusual steps in order to reach the poor, including outdoor preaching in the fields and streets, and the use of lay (unordained) preachers. Many of the innovations that became Methodist characteristics originated in the desire of the movement's leaders to reach the most neglected and marginalized members of society. London's slums, Bristol's docks, and impoverished mining communities like Kingswood became John Wesley's second and third homes. Wherever the poor gathered, so did the Methodists.

The history of Methodism likely would have amounted to little more than a minor paragraph in the larger history of Christian piety had Wesley not linked his heartwarming experience with a ministry to the poor. But Wesley took as his own the mission statement of his Master: "The Spirit of the Lord is upon me, because he hath anointed me to preach the gospel to the poor" (Luke 4:18, KJV).

By the 1740s Methodism had become a glowing revival flame spreading through the British Isles. The Methodist faithful gathered in small discipleship groups to nourish their spiritual lives. They preached and testified to their faith. At the same time they started new schools, tended to the sick, cared for orphans, and distributed medicine, food, and clothes. The growing Methodist network became an agent of spiritual, moral, and physical healing.

Concern for the downtrodden remained part of Wesley's outlook to the very end of his life. His last letter, written on his deathbed, urged William Wilberforce, a promising young politician, to take up the cause of abolishing slavery in the British Empire. Wilberforce accepted the challenge and devoted the rest of his life to that struggle. He became the leading abolitionist of his day and always enjoyed the unwavering support of British Methodists in this great cause.

The Wesleyan-Holiness Churches

American Methodism's relationship to slavery was not as exemplary as its British counterpart's, however. Following Wesley's sentiments, the Methodist Episcopal Church stated its opposition to slavery at the time that it organized in Baltimore in 1784. Almost immediately, however, it backed away from that commitment under the influence of slaveholding Methodists in the South and the imminent threat of schism. By 1840 the M.E. Church was officially mute on the divisive issue of slavery. One of today's Wesleyan-Holiness denominations came into existence precisely in reaction to that situation.

The Wesleyan Methodist Connection emerged in 1843 under the leadership of an abolitionist minister named Orange Scott. Scott originally was a minister in the M.E. Church's New England Conference, where he sought to awaken the consciences of fellow Methodists against slavery. At one point he purchased subscriptions to an abolitionist paper for each minister in the conference. Eventually he launched his own paper, *The True Wesleyan,* to advocate his view that "true Wesleyans" should work for the liberation of the slaves.

He and like-minded Methodists concluded after the General Conference of 1840 that antislavery reform was impossible within the main branch of Methodism. They decided to break away, form their own connection of churches, and labor unhindered in the abolition cause. Thus the oldest Wesleyan-Holiness denomination in America was born out of commitment to a great social cause.

The rich heritage of the Wesleys and early Methodism is shared in other ways by Wesleyan-Holiness churches. One of these—the Salvation Army—has shaped its inner life around a mission to the poor more fully than any other church in history.

The Salvation Army began in London's slums, founded by William and Catherine Booth. Its original name was the Christian Mission, and it functioned initially as an evangelistic agency. However, William Booth's perspective gradually changed as he evangelized among the poor. The Booths began to incorporate social work into their ministry. Eventually they reorganized the ministry under the name Salvation Army, concluding that military type discipline was vital to sustain the work of religious and social reform among the urban poor. In 1890 William Booth published his analysis of England's social problems, *In Darkest England, and the Way Out*—a book advocating broad social reform.

The Salvation Army came to be characterized by evangelistic street meetings and soup kitchens, vibrant worship in rented halls and the distribution of food and clothing, strong holiness preaching and literacy programs, and dozens of other expressions of compassion in Christ's name. Over the years it has remained true to the vision of its founders, and like early Methodism it aims at spiritual, moral, and physical healing. It can be found today on every inhabited continent, working to shelter the homeless or to mitigate gang violence. The urban poor remain the primary focus of its ministry.

Phoebe Palmer was the remarkable Methodist laywoman sometimes referred to as the Mother of the Ameri-

can Holiness Movement. She, too, exemplified the union
of vital piety and social concern. Palmer is remembered
primarily for her preaching, writing, and general leadership of the first phase of the 19th-century Holiness revival.
Palmer was also one of the leaders in a project sponsored
by Methodist women that established the Five Points Mission in New York City's slums. The Five Points Mission
rescued young girls from lives of prostitution, operated a
day school for poor children, arranged adoptions, fought
the saloon trade, and conducted worship. A large five-sto-
ry building was erected in 1853 to house these ministries
and more, including the distribution of clothing and a library used by workingmen in the evenings.

Others imitated the Five Points Mission in the Wesleyan-Holiness Movement. Theodore and Manie Ferguson,
for instance, founded the Peniel Mission in the Los Angeles slums in 1894. Like the Five Points Mission, the Peniel
Mission was housed in a substantial building and provided
a wide range of relief to the homeless and the poor. Peniel
Missions eventually were established in most major cities
of the West Coast.

The antislavery impulse that spawned the Wesleyan
Methodist Connection was also a motivation of Benjamin
Titus Roberts, founder of the Free Methodist Church.
However, Roberts also dissented from the Methodist Episcopal Church for another reason. He strongly objected to
pew rentals—a method that city churches increasingly
used to raise money. Pew rentals discriminated against the
poor. The well-to-do reserved the best seats in the sanctuary. Those who could not afford to rent pews sat in less
desirable seats. The very practice cried "Unwelcome!" to
the poor.

Roberts urged his congregation in Rochester, New York,
to change its practice. His laypeople refused. Roberts then
urged the Methodist churches across the city to cooperate
in planting one or more "free" churches. Even that did not

happen, so Roberts broke with the Methodist Church in 1860 and established the type of congregation he felt called of God to form. From the outset, the name Free Methodist was intended to convey two ideas: "freemen" (antislavery) and "free pews" (the poor were welcome in churches of this name).

Phineas Bresee was another who accepted the challenge of ministering to the needs of the urban poor. By 1894 Bresee had served every large Methodist church around Los Angeles as the area district superintendent. In that year he asked to be appointed to inner-city mission work. The request was refused, so Bresee stepped aside from the Methodist ministry.

For a year he served as the Sunday morning preacher at the Peniel Mission. Then he joined others to launch a new church in downtown Los Angeles. J. P. Widney, a physician, suggested the name Church of the Nazarene, pointing out that it identified the congregation with "the toiling, lowly mission of Christ."[1]

The congregation met in rented halls for several months before constructing a simple board church that was soon dubbed "the Glory Barn." Bresee said, "We want places so plain that every board says welcome to the poorest." He continued: "Let the Church of the Nazarene be true to its commission; not great and elegant buildings; but to feed the hungry and clothe the naked, and wipe away the tears of sorrowing; and gather jewels for His diadem."[2]

Seth C. Rees, an evangelical Quaker, was another Holiness revivalist who ministered to social outcasts and inspired others to do so. Urban poverty turned some young girls toward prostitution, so Rees inspired a small network of homes for unwed mothers known as Rest Cottages. The network was small but spanned the United States. Wesleyan Methodists, Nazarenes, and others sponsored various homes in this chain. A similar ministry was organized in Texas by J. T. Upchurch, whose Berachah Rescue Soci-

ety reached out to errant girls in the slums of Dallas, Fort
Worth, and Waco.

Other Wesleyan-Holiness denominations have shown
their commitment to the welfare of others through their
concerted efforts at peacemaking. The Evangelical Friends
and the Brethren in Christ both have roots in the Christian pacifist tradition. Both denominations incorporated
the primary emphasis of the Wesleyan-Holiness revival into their identities in the late 19th century.

At one time they saw their role as peace churches in
terms of refraining from war. Today they see peacemaking
as something active, rather than reactive. They teach conflict resolution and sponsor ministries that reconcile people and groups to one another. Norval Hadley, an Evangelical Friend, played a key role in the New Call to
Peacemaking that reenergized the peace churches in the
1970s. During the same period Ron Sider of the Brethren
in Christ focused the eyes of many Christians to the problem of world hunger in his best-selling book, *Rich Christians in an Age of Hunger.*

A Kingdom People

There are several reasons why Christians should care
for the bodies, as well as the spirits, of others. However,
the primary reason is that we should be, as Paul urged us,
"imitators . . . of Christ" (1 Corinthians 11:1, NASB).

Luke records the beginning of Jesus' ministry in 4:14-
21. At the synagogue in Nazareth, Jesus was handed the
Isaiah scroll. He read a portion that indicated God's love
for those who are forsaken. "The Spirit of the Lord is on
me, because he has anointed me to preach good news to
the poor. He has sent me to proclaim freedom for the prisoners and recovery of sight for the blind, to release the op-
pressed, to proclaim the year of the Lord's favor" (vv. 18-
19). It was no accident that, near the outset of His
ministry, He read and commented upon these particular

verses. They summed up the heart of His ministry to people.

In Luke 7:11-23 we see Jesus going about His remarkable ministry and John the Baptist's disciples coming to check Him out. Jesus' response to them shows that His ministry was properly focused on the most needy in society. "Report to John what you have seen and heard: The blind receive sight, the lame walk, those who have leprosy are cured, the deaf hear, the dead are raised, and the good news is preached to the poor" (v. 22).

The healing stories in the ministry of Jesus provide great insight into the character of God and the nature of God's kingdom. The compassionate works of Jesus toward the blind, the lame—even the dead—were not intended to be merely vivid demonstrations of power. There were, after all, other miracle workers in that day. Rather, they were unmistakable, obvious signs of God's kingdom breaking into history. Jesus' answer to the disciples of John the Baptist pointed toward the righteousness of His acts of mercy, not just to the power with which He accomplished them. The kingdom of God has its very basis in God's great love!

When Jesus returned to the One whom He called His "Father in heaven," He left behind His Church to carry on His ministry of reconciliation. It is now *our* mission to announce how God's kingdom breaks into human affairs. When Christians feed the hungry, care for the sick, provide for orphans and widows, or educate the illiterate in Christ's name, we are showing the world that the kingdom of God is at hand—that it is here, among us, right now.

We are already participating, in all likelihood, in some form of social ministry—at least indirectly. When we give tithes and offerings to our local churches, for instance, a portion of that goes to support missionaries who provide medical assistance and teach basic literacy in parts of the world where these are sorely needed. Some of our tithe may also support church-based orphanages, inner-city rescue missions, soup kitchens, or facilities for unwed mothers in far-flung places.

Still, the call to discipleship urges us to something deeper than only indirect ministry. We are called as Christians to be God's ministers in the world. Our pastors are called to equip us for ministry, but we—the people of God—are God's hands and feet at this particular point in human history.

Look around at your own congregation. Is it a place where the hungry or the homeless would turn in their need? If so, then why? If not, then why not? Would your congregation's testimony to the wider community be more credible or less credible if it was involved more deeply in some form of social ministry?

Some Wesleyan-Holiness congregations have started new social ministries over the past two decades when "mission groups" have formed within congregations. In some cases, mission groups have started ministries to those dying of AIDS. Other mission groups have worked in soup kitchens, participated with Christians of other denominations in building low-cost homes, or served as conflict mediators.

The redemptive work of God through Christ frees us from sin and sets us free to serve others. The ways in which we can do so are as unbounded as the sea of human need.

Background Scripture: Luke 4:14-21; 7:11-23

About the Author: Dr. Stan Ingersol is a church historian and the archivist for the international Church of the Nazarene in Kansas City.

NOTES

1. Timothy L. Smith, *The Story of the Nazarenes: The Formative Years,* vol. 1 of *Called unto Holiness* (Kansas City: Nazarene Publishing House, 1962), 111.

2. Phineas Bresee, editorial, *Nazarene Messenger,* January 15, 1902, 6.

CHAPTER 13

How Do I Plug In?

by David Kendall

In this book we have sought to hear the call of God on our lives. The fact is: God calls all of us to "full-time Christian service"—24 hours each day, 7 days each week. Nothing less than full-time does justice to His call. Nothing other than service, or ministry, can be the outcome.

Let me remind you that in the beginning of the Church there were only laypersons. The first human leaders—the apostles—about whom we usually have pastoral thoughts and feelings, were anything but pastor types. What were they? Fishermen, tax collectors, political activists, owners and operators of small family businesses, and the like. In other words, when they were around, it was not incense from the Temple you smelled!

The apostle Paul cut to the heart of the matter when he described the Christians in Corinth—leaders and followers alike—in these terms:

> Brothers, think of what you were when you were called. Not many of you were wise by human standards; not many were influential; not many were of noble birth. But God chose the foolish things of the world to shame the wise; God chose the weak things of the world to shame the strong. He chose the lowly things of this world and the despised things—and the things that are not—to nullify the things that are, so that no one may boast before him. It is because of him that you are in Christ Jesus, who has become for us wisdom from

God—that is, our righteousness, holiness and redemption. Therefore, as it is written: "Let him who boasts boast in the Lord" *(1 Corinthians 1:26-31).*

In other words, according to the standards of this world, all of them were equally unqualified to do anything. Yet, God called *all of them* to do great things for His kingdom. As another translation puts verse 30, God "is the source of your life in Christ Jesus" (NRSV). Because He is, His call to serve in great ways comes to all of us.

As a matter of fact, God has never chosen the world's bright, shining stars for His most impressive works in history. In the entire Bible we see God tapping the most unlikely and unsuspecting folks to fulfill the most amazing roles. Think of some of the Old Testament examples—Noah, Abram and Sarai, Jacob, Joseph, Moses, Gideon, Deborah, Samuel, Ruth, David, and Esther, to name just a few. Sometimes we allow the later story of what God did through these people to overshadow how unlikely and incompetent they seem at the beginning. All the way through history, in the Bible and the Church, God has used ordinary people for extraordinary purposes. This is the rule, not the exception.

God continues to call all of His people, including us, to do extraordinary work for His kingdom. History should be enough to convince us that no deficiencies in background, no failures in our past, and no supposed lack in ability should stand in the way of our being effective and joyful servants of God in our everyday lives.

Still, how do we plug in? How do we become the full-time Christian servants Christ calls us to be? For the most part, the answers come in having the right perspective and in offering God ready obedience.

Having the Right Perspective

One word will help us focus—God. Most of the problems we have with seeing ourselves as competent and effective servants of God traces back to the wrong focus. Too often our focus is on *us,* not on God. Focusing on self can lead to two different roadblocks to being God's people.

Perhaps the most common roadblock is to take a low view of ourselves. We may say, "Who am I to do great things for God? I lack the talent and training. I'm too young. I'm too old. I'm not like so and so. I have this or that limitation." We all know how convincing these arguments can be.

A classic example of taking a low view of self is the children of Israel. God had delivered them from slavery in Egypt for new life in a Land of Promise. In the process of delivering them, God demonstrated His awesome power. Yet, when the time came to enter the land, the people forgot God's power and focused on their weakness. Most of the spies Moses sent to scout out the land reported that the people in the land were numerous and strong. As a result, they seemed like grasshoppers to themselves and to their enemies (see Numbers 13—14). When we focus on ourselves, especially in light of what we know God is asking us to do, we may indeed seem small and insignificant.

A second roadblock we may meet when we focus on ourselves lies in the other direction. It is possible for us to overestimate our abilities and to think more highly of ourselves than we should. We imagine that God got a pretty good deal when He got us. We're ready to take on the world for Jesus, whatever the challenge. Indeed, some of us in our own strength may meet many challenges successfully, but the outcome will not please God if self is the focus.

God must be the focus. We must keep clearly in mind who God is and what He has revealed about himself and His plans for the world, as well as for us.

When God is our focus, we will remember that He is the Creator. He is the One who made the universe out of nothing, on the sheer strength of His word. Hebrews says, "By faith we understand that the universe was formed at

God's command, so that what is seen was not made out of what was visible" (11:3). *This* is the God who calls us to himself and into His full-time service. With God as our focus, questions of competence and ability fall silent.

If God calls us to do something, He provides the power we need, even if it seems impossible to us. When God called Moses to speak His word of deliverance to the children of Israel, and to Pharaoh on their behalf, Moses complained of a "slow tongue." God replied, in effect, "Who do you think made that tongue?" (see Exodus 4:10-12). When God's angel appeared to Mary to announce her pregnancy, Mary noted the biological impossibility of what God was proposing. The angel reminded her, "Nothing is impossible with God" (Luke 1:37). When the first followers of Jesus turned the world upside down (or right side up), the religious authorities "took note that [they] had been with Jesus" (Acts 4:13). If our focus is on God, the Creator, then His call to serve Him, whatever its details, will never seem out of reach to us. Indeed, His call is the best guarantee we have of all the power we could ever need.

God, the Creator, is also Redeemer. Human rebellion, which unleashed the power of sin and its consequences on the world, has made a wreck of God's creative plans. Still, God acts as Savior and Redeemer to salvage His world and people. As part of His saving plans for the world, He calls people to belong to Him and to be His servants. He told the children of Israel, "Now if you [will] obey me fully and keep my covenant, then out of all nations you will be my treasured possession. Although the whole earth is mine, you will be for me a kingdom of priests and a holy nation" (Exodus 19:5-6). Likewise, Peter applies this promise to followers of Jesus: "But you are a chosen people, a royal priesthood, a holy nation, a people belonging to God, that you may declare the praises of him who called you out of darkness into his wonderful light" (1 Peter 2:9).

In other words, God saves us to become His servants, who live and work in the world for His honor and glory. Thus, at the heart of our salvation we find God's concern to make us participants in His loving reach around the whole world. Everyone whom God saves plays a role in this plan. At least that is what God intends!

If our focus is on God the Redeemer, we will know that serving God—being a "minister"—is not an option or an add-on we will do if we can find the time and the right position opens up. No, being a minister is simply one of several ways to describe what we are when we belong to God.

God, the Creator and Redeemer, comes to clear and powerful focus for us in Jesus. He was the very "image of God" (2 Corinthians 4:4) and expressed the exact likeness of God. As such, Jesus took action to bring a new order to life. "Therefore, if anyone is in Christ, he is a new creation" (5:17). As we have seen, our life in Christ has its source in God (1 Corinthians 1:30).

When God is our focus, as we see Him in Jesus, we can't help but understand the kind of people God wants us to be. Jesus was the servant of God, "who, being in very nature God, did not consider equality with God something to be grasped, but made himself nothing, taking the very nature of a servant, being made in human likeness" (Philippians 2:6-7). Jesus said of himself, "For even the Son of Man did not come to be served, but to serve, and to give his life as a ransom for many" (Mark 10:45).

Jesus' call to follow Him is, therefore, a call to be servants. "As you [the Father] have sent me, so I have sent them into the world," His disciples heard Him pray (see John 17:18). Certainly He was not a part-time servant of God! He was full-time. So are His followers, when they keep Him as their focus.

When God is our focus, as we see Him in Jesus, we have access to the power we need to be full-time servants as Jesus was. He has given us the promise of His Spirit.

"You will receive power when the Holy Spirit comes on you; and you will be my witnesses" (Acts 1:8). To every one of us God has given His Spirit and His grace to serve Him and others (Ephesians 4:7-12). His Spirit creates a community—the Church, His Body on earth. In the Church, each of us has a role to play. In concert with one another, we grow and mature as servants who become a community of ministers. Jesus is the Head of this community and supplies the power necessary for us to be who He calls us to be—together and individually.

If our focus is on God our Creator and Redeemer, as He reveals himself in Jesus, we will have the right perspective and will settle the matter for ourselves. God has all the power we will ever need to do what He calls us to do. Thus, when we hear His call to participate in His saving plans for the whole world, we will be confident that He will do it through us as we continue to walk with Jesus in the power of His Spirit. That is, He will if only we will allow.

Offering God Ready Obedience

Truly, obedience is the bottom line. The truths covered in this book challenge us primarily at the point of our obedience.

The sharp distinction between pastors and "the rest of the people" does not line up with God's will. Therefore, will we understand that we all have a full-time calling from God?

The realities of modern life often distract us and deceive us. We can make choices, perhaps not bad per se, that lead us to serve self or others, not God. A careful review of our personal habits and life patterns will often reveal where we are not truly serving God. Therefore, will we ask God to help us evaluate our lifestyle choices, our attitudes toward money, leisure, entertainment, employment, and career, and bring the whole of our lives into line with what He reveals?

God the Creator and Redeemer, at work in His people through Jesus and the Spirit, not only calls but also equips and empowers us to serve Him full-time. Therefore, will we take advantage of the spiritual gifts inventories available to us, seek understanding of those ways God has gifted us to serve, and then serve?

God's plan embraces the whole world, and we are called to be part of what He is doing. Therefore, will we seek to know where God is at work all around us and join Him by using our gifts and abilities to serve Him and others?

Will we obey? That's the bottom line. It's not a heavy, burdensome obedience. Rather, it's the natural response of people whose hearts well up with gratitude and joy in the Lord.

What a wonder it is to be loved by God, to be given new life, to be honored with something important to do in His eternal plan, and to be able to do it. Not because we are so great or deserving, but because God is so good! In this light, obedience to God's calling can be nothing other than a delight!

Background Scripture: Exodus 4:10-12; 19:5-6; Numbers 13—14; Mark 10:45; Luke 1:37; John 17:18; Acts 1:8; 4:13; 1 Corinthians 1:26-31; 2 Corinthians 4:4; 5:17; Ephesians 4:7-12; Philippians 2:6-7; Hebrews 11:3; 1 Peter 2:9

About the Author: Dr. David Kendall is former senior pastor of the Free Methodist church, McPherson, Kansas, and is currently superintendent of the Great Plains Conference of the Free Methodist Church.